VIRTUE BLOSSOMS LIKE FLOWERS

Common Destiny Teenagers' Series

Makhukhu John Tladi

To order additional copies of this book, contact:
Xlibris
1-888-795-4274
www.Xlibris.com
Orders@Xlibris.com

ISBN: Softcover   978-1-9845-8495-3
         EBook   978-1-9845-8494-6

Print information available on the last page

Rev. date: 06/26/2020

Contents

DEDICATION

I dedicated this book to my granddaughter Khanya Atlegang Tladi who was born on a Thursday the 07-02-2019. May the Good Lord take care of you my granddaughter and bless you in all you do! King Solomon wrote about children and said:

Don't you know that children are God's best gift? The fruit of the womb his generous legacy?

Like a warrior's fistful of arrows are the children of a vigorous youth

Oh, how blessed are your parents, with your quivers full of children!

"Your enemies don't stand a chance against you; you'll sweep them right off your doorstep".

(Psalm 127:3-5)

From your loving grand father

Pastor Makhukhu John Tladi

01-03-2020

FOREWORD

The purpose of this book is to guide and nurture teenagers or adolescents around the world to develop physically and psychologically so that they could become well-rounded God-fearing adults in future. They need to be taught appropriate godly values and life-skills to achieve this goal. They should always remember that they are our future world leaders who will take over when we are no more. However the greatest challenges facing humanity nowadays are huge and fearsome. We are drowning in a sea of impurity nowadays. Everywhere we look, we find temptations to lead impure lives. How do we stay pure and godly in a filthy environment? We cannot do this on our own, but must have council and strength more dynamic than the tempting influence around the world. Where can find that strength and wisdom by applying God's word and doing what it says.

A teenager or an adolescent is a person who falls within the age of 13-19 years. The word teenager is another word for an adolescent. They are still developing physically and psychologically. It is a time between being a child and a matured adult, that is the period of time during which a person grows into an adult, but they are emotionally not mature. But when they turn 20, they are no longer teenagers. The way this word is used varies from society to society. In the English language adolescents (people going through adolescence) are frequently called "teenagers" or "teens" which comes from the English words "thirteen" or "nineteen". This is a very critical developmental stage-a make or break stage because this is where the future is won or lost. And hiding (keeping) God's word in their hearts and learning appropriate virtues will be their long-lasting deterrents to sin and shame.

God's word is true and wonderful. Stay true to God and his word no matter how bad the world becomes. Obedience to God's law and practising good virtues is the only teenagers or adolescents can achieve real happiness. The Author of Psalm (119:9-16) summed up this truth when he said:

"How can a young man keep his way pure? By living according to your word.

I seek you with all my heart; do not let me stay from your commands

I have hidden your word in my heart that I might not sin against you.

Praise be to you, O Lord; teach me your decrees.

With my lips I recount all the laws that come from your mouth,

I rejoice in following your statues as one rejoices in great riches

I meditate on your precepts and consider your ways,

I delight in your decrees, I will not neglect your word".

Most of us chafe under rules and virtues are a strange phenomenon to many of us. We think that these basic rules and principles restrict us from doing what we want. But God's laws and principles were given to free us to be all he wants us to be. They restrict us from doing what might cripple us and keep us from being our best. But God's guidelines help us follow his path and avoid path that leads to destruction. Enjoy your reading and always make sure that your life shine like stars!

FOOD FOR THOUGHT

"The heart is the central organ which controls all man's activities, and so determines the character of his living. Salvation, after all is not a matter of living up to the code of ethics. It is a matter of the heart. After the heart is right with God, good conduct flows from its hidden springs. To train a child only in outward manners is not sufficient. He must be told of the inward sources of power which will direct him in the right path".

(C.T.Fritsch, The Interpreter's Bible, Vol. 4 P811)

WISDOM

GENERAL FEATURES

Reasoning

Discernment

Insight

Clear-headedness

Clear-sightedness

THE VIRTUE OF WISDOM BLOSSOM LIKE A FLOWER WHEN PROPERLY NURTURED

SO! MAKE A DECISION TODAY TO TAKE GOOD CARE OF IT.

VIRTUE NUMBER ONE: WISDOM

READ ON!

How does a teenager align his goals with God's? How does he become the kind of person God wants him to become? Take time to think about your dreams and goals, and make sure they cover the really important areas of your life. I arrived at the University of Limpopo in February 1975 armed with a seven months salvation experience and my senior certificate university exception results. I was very apprehensive because I did not know what to expect. But I held dearly to (Proverbs 21:24) basic teaching which says *"A discerning man keeps wisdom in view, but a fools' eyes wander to the end of the earth"*. This proverb points out the folly of chasing fantasies (having eyes that wonder to the ends of the earth) while losing the essence of the real thing. I heard about countess teenagers' testimonies who fell by the wayside and lost their academic and spiritual goals because they were (having eyes that wondered to the of the earth).I knew that I had to invent a workable strategy to guard my new found Christian faith against the prevalent dominating tertiary level philosophies and other world views and make sure that I succeed in my academic and my spiritual goals. I thank God who gave me a plan for success. He gave me wisdom and I managed to see the light through and through-Something I thought was not possible. I completed my studies in a record time. No supplementary and no fail. All glory goes to him because he made it all possible.

Prior to the resumption of the 1975 academic year, I visited the university during September 1974 with my fellow Christian friend. We accompanied our college soft ball team to the high schools tournament even though we were not members of the college team. While the teams were competing against each in the stadium, we took time out to conduct prayer walks around the campus. We did our spiritual mapping thoroughly and we were satisfied that we reached our goals. I visited the university one Monday morning prior to the 1975 academic year's resumption to conduct my second prayer walks again. I gave myself time to walk about alone in silence and visualise my future Christian life and my studies. God gave me a winning formula there and then and up to this day I am still applying the same strategy wherever I come across new challenging situations. This is now my blue-print for success. I decided to buy a nice blue badge written "Jesus Saves" and put it on my shirt on the registration day. This was a giant step indeed because I was just about to go through a meaningful self-actualization process: from high school teenager to a university student.

The "Jesus Saves" badge gave me so much confidence that before the end of the registration day, I had already attracted the attention of two young first year students. We became friends and began to share our faith while registering. We managed to attend the first Students Christian Movement Prayer meeting at 18h00. We met other Christian students on campus and that meeting made me to solidify my resolves that I will succeed in all I was going to do for the next four years. Namely, study hard and pray hard. I then took off my badge and put it in my suite case because I had accomplished my mission. I had planted enough roots to sustain me and these roots began to grow and develop. I had one focus and one mission only-develop spiritually and academically. Thank God that this simple wisdom kept me safe and sound until I completed my studies successfully. I always felt pity for so many of my student folks who used to lose direction and become discouraged. I finally ended up becoming a Student Advisor to help my fellow students. Virtues such as wisdom, honesty, patience and love may not seem exciting, but they will ultimately determine your eternal future.

WHAT IS WISDOM

Consider the following statement: *"A decision not to take illegal drugs because of the data showing the destructive effects of so doing is a wise decision and prevents heartache for the decision maker and those of their circle of influence".* Every day we journey on this earth is a day in which we make choices left and right, up and down, in or out, yes or noisome choices are simple, and some are very complex. But we have to make those choices. Who will we trust to see us through this journey? Who will be our guide? Wisdom, wisdom and wisdom. Wisdom is a very important virtue and all humans should pray and strive to possess it. Wisdom means a comprehensive knowledge that is put into practice. Wisdom is the state of being wise. Humans need wisdom to be able to survive in today's tough and rough world. Other words describing wisdom are: Insight, discernment, clear-sightedness and clear-headedness. Wisdom enables you to make good decisions that are both good for you and for others. It enables you know when to act, how to act and how to balance your other different virtues when they are in conflict. Solomon describes wisdom as a gift from God. *"The lord gives wisdom and from his mouth come knowledge and understanding".* (Prov.2:6)

Being wise means being be able to discern as to how to act after you have digested, data or information and circumstances before you. Intelligence and wisdom are not the same gifts. An individual may have great intellect and being armed with a wealth of information and still make wrong decisions. A wise person is able to synthesise all the information available to him before making proper decisions. He is patient and takes time to weigh all the facts available to him before making a solid decision and his decisions are always right.

SOLOMON: THE WISE KING

King Solomon is regarded as the wisest man who ever lived. Solomon means "peaceful" and his parents were King David and Bathsheba. King Solomon was a peaceful king. Unlike his father David, he did not fight wars. He had a good sense to recognise his need for wisdom when he was still a teenager. He prayed to God and said: *"I am only a little child and do not know how to carry out my duties....Give your servant a discerning heart to govern your people and to distinguish between right and wrong".* The Lord granted him his wish and gave him *"A wise and a discerning heart"* to enable him to carry out his duties responsibly. His vision encourages us to do the same.

But it was up to King Solomon to apply that God given wisdom to all areas of his life. The one aspect that made him to fail as a leader was that he did not want to go to war like his father David did. He preferred to adopt a diplomatic strategy where he forged relationships by marrying foreign wives-Something God did not allow him and the nation of Israel to do. He was obviously wise in governing the nation of Israel, but he was foolish in running own household. *He had seven hundred wives of royal birth and three hundred concubines and his wives led him astray.* (1Ki.11:1-6).This wayward behaviour ultimately led to his demise when he was old. However his settlement of a dispute between two prostitutes (1 Ki. 3:16-28) was a classic example of his wisdom. This wise ruling was verification that God had answered his prayer and gave him a discerning heart. King Solomon's gift of wisdom enabled him to become a well organised administrator. According to (1Ki.4:1-19) he had eleven officials with specific responsibilities.

He had twelve district governors and a manager in charge of the district officers. Each official had a specific territory to manage. This kind of administrative arrangement was very innovative indeed and was very essential for the maintenance of an effective government structure. It was a wise move by a wise leader. The fruits of his wisdom were peace, security and prosperity for his nation. His government era is often looked upon as the ideal of what any nation can become when united in trust and obedience to God. The book of Proverbs records many of his 3,000 wise sayings. Other Biblical wise writings written by him are: Psalm (72:1-17) and Psalm (127:1-5) Song of Songs and Ecclesiastes.

SOURCES OF WISDOM

WISDOM IS A GIFT FROM GOD

"The Lord gives wisdom, and from his mouth come knowledge and understanding". (Proverbs 2:6)

God gives us wisdom, knowledge, understanding and victory, but not for drifting through life or acting irresponsibly with his gifts and resources. If we are faithful and keep our purpose in life clearly in mind, he will keep us from pride and greed. But if we forget our purpose, we will surely fall.

WISDOM IS A GIFT FROM THE SPIRIT

"Now to each one the manifestation of the spirit is given for the common good". To one there is given through the same spirit the message of wisdom, to another the message of knowledge by means of the same spirit (1 Cor.12:7-8)

God gives us wisdom and knowledge through his spirit. This is an unusual gift indeed but all humans are free to ask for it and they will receive it. It is very interesting to observe that the very same spirit that gives us wisdom can give us other gifts such as gift of faith, healing, miraculous powers, prophesy and the gift of distinguishing between spirits.

WISDOM STARTS WITH THE FEAR OF THE LORD

"The fear of the Lord is the beginning of wisdom and knowledge of the holy one is understanding". (Proverbs 9:10)

Wisdom starts with the knowledge of knowing God. To know God is not just to know the facts about him but to stand in awe of him and to have a personal relationship with him. Wisdom starts with respect for God. It leads to right living and results in increased ability to tell right from wrong. Do you really want to be wise? Then get to know God better and believe in him.

WISDOM COMES FROM RESEARCH AND EDUCATION

"So I turned my mind to understand, to investigate and to search out wisdom and the scheme of things, and to understand the stupidity of wickedness and the madness of folly". (Eccl.7:25)

Nothing in the world can substitute experience, knowledge and understanding. This is true with wisdom acquisition. You need continuous research and balanced education to acquire it.

King Solomon the wisest man in the world confessed how difficult it had been to act and think wisely. He emphasised that no matter how much we know, there always mysteries we will never understand. So do not get tired of engaging yourself in research and education and never think that you have enough wisdom, knowledge and understanding.

WISDOM COMES FROM DISCIPLINE

The rod of correction imparts wisdom, but a child left to him disgraces his mother (Prov. 29:15)

Parents of young children often weary of disciplining them. The feel like all they do is nag, scold and punish again and again. If you have ruined every chance for a loving relationship with them, remember this kind firm correction helps them to learn and learning makes them wise. Consistent loving discipline will ultimately teach them to discipline themselves.

WISDOM COMES FROM ADMONISHING ONE ANOTHER

"Let the word of Christ dwell in you richly as you teach and admonish one another with all wisdom, and as you sing psalms, hymns and spiritual songs with gratitude in your hearts to God" (Colossians 3:16).

We acquire wisdom through reprimanding and teaching one another. The early Christians used this knowledge acquisition method very effectively. Although the early church had access to the Old Testament and freely used it, they did not yet have the New Testament or any other Christian books to study. Their stories and teachings about Jesus Christ were memorised and passed on from person to person. They admonished and taught each other through psalms, spiritual songs and hymns. Music became an important part of their Christian worship and education. They acquired wisdom.

LIFE-SKILLS LESSONS

We may draw the following life-skills lessons from this very important first virtue: These are:

- Wisdom is an important virtue because wise decisions often prevent heartaches. Wisdom can prevent difficult situations from developing or getting worse. A wise person possesses God given abilities and can read between the lines and avoid the danger before it strikes.

- The gift of wisdom is available to all humans. It is available to you too and you can access it through prayer. So! Dedicate your life to God. But unlike King Solomon, you must put it into action and make sure that it works for you and for your fellow humans. Applying wisdom to life demonstrate that you possess discernment abilities

- But the danger is, you might lose it cheaply too. This was true to King Solomon's God give wisdom. He started very well as a wise leader but lost it when he grew older. While he became a famous builder of the temple and the palace, he became infamous as a leader who excessively taxed and worked his people. Visitors from distant countries came to admire this wise king while his own people were gradually alienated from him. The beautiful rare gift God gave him did not safe him and he died without hope and dignity.

- King Solomon reigned in Jerusalem over all Israel for forty years. Then he rested with his fathers and as buried in the city of David his father. And Rehoboam his son succeeded him.

SELF-ASSESSMENT ON WISDOM

GIFTING	LOW	AVERAGE	GOOD
• My reasoning skill is?			
• My discernment skill is?			
• My insightfulness skill is?			
• My clear-headedness skill is?			
• My clear-sightedness skill is?			

ACTION POINTS

I will improve and maintain wisdom by:

1.	
2.	
3.	
4.	
5.	

DAILY SCRIPTURES ON: THE BENEFITS OF WISDOM

(To inspire and guide you as you go about your daily business)

DAY 1:Wisdom makes us blessed: *"Blessed is the man who finds wisdom, the man who gains understanding"* (Proverbs 3:13).

DAY 2:*"Do not be wise in your own eyes; fear the Lord and shun evil* (Proverbs 3:7).

Day 3:*"Wisdom is the shelter as money is a shelter, but the advantage of knowledge is this; that wisdom preserves the life of its possessor".* (Ecclesiastes 7:12)

DAY 4:*"Better one handful with tranquillity than two hands with toil and chasing after the wind".* (Proverbs 4:6)

DAY 5:*"Wisdom makes one wise man more powerful than ten rulers in a city".* (Ecclesiastes 7:19)

DAY 6:*"A man, who loves wisdom, brings joy to his father, but a companion of prostitutes squanders his wealth".* (Proverbs 29:3)

DAY 7:*"Getting wisdom is the most important thing you can do. Whatever else you get, insight".* (Proverbs 4:7)

JUSTICE

GENERAL FEATURES

Uprightness

Honourableness

Conscientiousness

Impartiality

Fairness

THE VIRTUE OF JUSTICE BLOSSOM LIKE A FLOWER WHEN PROPERLY NURTURED

SO! MAKE A DECISION TODAY TO TAKE GOOD CARE OF IT

VIRTUE NUMBER TWO: JUSTICE

READ ON!

Young people are encouraged to practice justice in all they say and do nowadays because: *"when justice is done, it brings joy to the righteous but terror to the evil doers"* (Proverbs 21:15).There is a great concern for justice in our world today and teenagers all over the world are encouraged to live in harmony and peace with each other. They are encouraged not be haughty but that they should always associate with the lowly. They should never be wise in their own sight and should repay no one evil with evil but that they should always give thought to what is good and honourable in the sight of all. Moses give us comfort (Deut.16:20) when he wrote many centuries ago and said *"Justice and only justice, you shall follow so that you may inherit the land that the Lord your God is giving you"*. However, to achieve justice for the world teenagers should understand how God views justice.

I undertook a marketing drive journey to Penge Mine area one Friday morning. I visited several schools in the mountainous Leolo area until 15h00 in the afternoon. On my way back home I gave one lady teacher a lift. She was staying in Seshego Township some 157km away. I asked her to pay me R50-00 for the trip and she did not have it at that moment. We agreed that we would stop at Nedbank in Polokwane city to allow her to do her withdrawal. We got into a normal passenger-driver discussion when she suddenly looked at me and said:

"I need protection because every time I withdraw money from the automatic teller machine young teenager thugs just come and take my money away. I need protection, protection, protection".

"How do these young thugs identify you because we are now 157km. away from Polokwane"?

I asked.

"I do not know but all I know is that every time I withdraw money they are in the vicinity and they just rob me and disappear. I need protection, protection and more protection".

I looked straight at her and said: "I do not believe your story but I will make sure that this does not happen to you today".

I felt very strongly inside my heart that this was injustice in the true sense of the word. Young thugs have no right to rob poor people in this manner. But I also felt very strongly that she was her own victim nonetheless. She was suffering from a severe inferiority complex syndrome and her tertiary education and training could not liberate her from her continuous injustice miseries. I am a senior citizen now and I have never entertained any idea whereby someone could rob me of my hard earned precious money and it never happened to me. When the Devil is at work, he does not care about our educational standards or our cultural backgrounds. His purpose is only to *"steal, to kill and to destroy"* (John 10:10).We finally arrived at the automatic teller machine in Polokwane and we found three people waiting to withdraw money. Our turn finally came and I stood close to her to witness what she has been telling me all the way through our journey. She processed everything and we waited for the money to come out. All of a sudden a young untidy teenager appeared from nowhere and shouted in a loud voice and said:

"Mam! That machine is faulty!"

"It is going to rob you!"

"It is going to take your money away!"

Suddenly she left all her money in the automatic teller machine with fear written all over her face, pushed me one side and said to the young untidy teenager:

"Is that so?"

"Yes "He replied.

I quickly jumped into action and blocked the untidy teenager with my one hand while I quickly removed the money from the machine. I put my life on line and acted as if I was one of the law enforcement officers. The young teenager realised that danger was looming and he ran as fast as he could. I am still struggling to figure out what was really happening here. How can other people be so mean with the result that they find it easy to steal, kill and destroy? On the other hand, how can so many people stoop so low that they become victims of fear and inferiority complex? That is no true?

WHAT IS JUSTICE

Read the following statement: *"It is amazing how quickly we shift from longing for justice to expecting mercy. If God's people are to do 'justice and mercy' as prophet Micah puts it, neither of these things will be hard to understand. But it is challenging to practice both of them at the same time".* Practicing true justice may come to our rescue in this regard because it teaches us what is right and just. Justice is an important virtue and all humans should strive to possess it and apply in all they do. Justice is the implementation of fairness in the treatment of others. Other words describing justice are: Uprightness, honourableness, morality, straightness and lawfulness. Justice enables us to respect the rights of all people regardless of their race, sex, religion, creed, colour and cultural backgrounds. Justice makes us to accept the fact that we are all humans and that we are all equal. The four types of justice are:

- COMMUNICATIVE JUSTICE: It is based on the principle of equality and informs us that we are all equal. We are all created in God's image and we should all receive equal treatment regardless of our race, religion, cultural background and the rest.

- DISTRIBUTIVE JUSTICE: It guarantees the common welfare of all people by sharing what God has created for all his people. We should share equally what God has created for all of us regardless of our race, culture, religion and the rest

- LEGAL JUSTICE: It informs us about the government's obligations and responsibilities towards its citizens. We should all receive equal protection and service from the government regardless of our race, culture, religion and the rest

- SOCIAL JUSTICE: It informs us that everybody has a right to a fair say and equal treatment in the society. We all have the right to a fair say and equal treatment before the law regardless of our race, colour, religion, cultural background and the rest.

Justice involves fairness in the treatment of others. It involves creating an environment wherein individuals, communities and the whole cosmos can feel safe and secured. Justice starts at the centre of true religion. James emphasised the importance of justice when he said," *Religion that God our Father accepts as pure and faultless is this; to look after orphans and widows in their distress and to keep oneself from being polluted by the world*". (James 1:27).We need to commit ourselves to Christ's ethical and moral standards and not to the world's. We are not to adapt to the world's value system which is based on money, power and pleasure. True faith means nothing if we are contaminated with such values. *"God is just. He will pay back trouble to those who trouble you and give relief to you who are troubled, and to us as well"*. (2 Thessalonians 2:6-7)

PROPHET NATHAN: MAN OF JUSTICE

Prophet Nathan was an embodiment of justice. He lived up to the meaning of his name. "He (God) has given". He proved himself as a fearless counsellor, always willing to speak and to stand for the truth even when he knew great pain would result. In confronting King David's multiple sins of coveting, theft, adultery and murder and in his affair with Bathsheba, Nathan was able to help David see his own wrongdoing by showing that he would not have tolerated such actions from anyone else. He defended Uriah and Bathsheba's right and prevailed against the mighty king. King David's repentance allowed Prophet Nathan to comfort him with the reality of God's forgiveness, and at the same time reminds him of the painful consequences his sin would bring. He saved King David and Bathsheba as well as their child who died later. God forgave King David for his sinful action. But he also comforted Bathsheba from her grieve because she lost her husband Uriah under mysterious circumstances. David and Bathsheba finally married each other and they became a husband and wife.

Prophet Nathan's approach helps us judge our own actions. How often do we make wrong choices and condemn others for making such choices? It is helpful to ask ourselves how God and others see our actions. Unfortunately, we have a huge capacity to lie to ourselves and prevent truth and justice to prevail. You are holding God's word. Let it speak to you about yourself even if the truth is painful. Let it help you to implement peace and justice in all you say and do. If you do not have a friend like Prophet Nathan, ask God for one. And ask God to use you as a suitable Nathan for someone else. Remember! *"As those justified by faith in the God of all justice, we are to experience the wholeness that he brings and extend it as citizens of the kingdom"*. Prophet Nathan story is told in (2 Samuel 11-12).He is also mentioned in (1 Chronicles 17:15, 2 Chronicles 9:29; 29:25)

LIFE-SKILLS LESSONS

We may draw the following life-skills lessons from this second important virtue

- Prophet Nathan brought about justice for all. King David was saved from his sins and wrongdoings. His faith was ultimately restored (Psalm 51:1-19).He ultimately married Bathsheba and King Solomon was born and he became Israel's third king. Bathsheba's faith was restored even though she lost her husband Uriah under mysterious circumstances. Her name is mentioned in Jesus genealogy (Matthew 1:6).People all over the world need justice and fairness. We can draw valuable lessons from Prophet Nathan's strategy and apply it effectively in our own circumstance.

- Prophet Nathan brought about forgiveness between God, King David and Bathsheba. Forgiveness involves (Romans 12:19-21) both attitude and actions. If you find it difficult to feel forgiving towards someone who has hurt you, try responding with kind actions. Tell this person that you would like to heal your relationship. Lend a helping hand. Send him a gift. Smile at him or her. Many a times you will discover that right actions lead to right feelings.

- Prophet Nathan was an agent of justice and mercy. He reconciled King David and Bathsheba with God. Prophet Zechariah (7:9-10) argued this point very strong when he said: *"Administer true justice, show mercy and compassion to one another. Do not oppress the widow of fatherless, the alien or the poor. In your hearts, do not think evil of each other"*.

- Prophet Nathan introduced restorative justice to King David and Bathsheba and to the world. Justice does not only to punish the evildoers and bring them to book. There is also a restorative aspect attached to it. Most of the time the Bible uses the word restorative justice in which those who are uprightly hurt or wronged are restored and given back what was taken away from them. Taken in this way, the combination of righteousness and justice that God dictates means a selfless life in which people are treated well and injustices are fixed.

- Justice form part of God's character and a person who calls himself God's follower should treat others justly. The beginning of justice is concern for what is happening to others. A Christian cannot be indifferent to human suffering because God isn't.

SELF-ASSESSMENT ON JUSTICE

GIFTING	LOW	AVERAGE	GOOD
• My uprightness skill is?			
• My honourableness skill is?			
• My consciousness skill is?			
• My impartiality skill is?			
• My fairness skill is?			

ACTION POINTS

I will improve and maintain justice by:

1.	
2.	
3.	
4.	
5.	

DAILY SCRIPTURES ON: THE BENEFITS OF JUSTICE

(To inspire you and guide you as you go about your daily business)

DAY 1: *"But let justice roll on like a river, righteousness like a never-failing stream"*. (Amos 5:24)

DAY 2: *"He has showed you! Man, what is good. And what does the Lord require of you? To act justly, to love mercy and to walk humbly with your God"*. (Micah 6:8)

DAY 3: *"Turn from evil and do good, then you will dwell in the land for ever. For the Lord loves the just and will not forsake his faithful once. They will be protected forever. But the offspring of the wicked will be cut off"*. (Psalm 37:27-29)

DAY 4: *"Learn to do right, seek justice, encourage the oppressed. Defend the cause of the fatherless, plead the case of the widow"*. (Isaiah 1:17)

DAY 5: *"He who pursues righteousness and love finds life, prosperity and honour"*. (Proverbs 28:15)

DAY 6: *"Evil men do not understand justice, but those who seek the Lord understand it fully"*. (Proverbs 28:5)

DAY 7: *"If it is possible as far as it depends on you, live at peace with everyone. Do not take revenge, my friends, but leave room for God's wrath, for it is written It is mine to avenge; I will repay "says the Lord"*.(Romans 12:19)

FORTITUDE

GENERAL FEATURES

Courage

Bravery

Daring

Boldness

Will-power

THE VIRTUE OF FORTITUDE BLOSSOM LIKE A FLOWER WHEN PROPERLY NURTURED

SO! MAKE A DECISION TODAY TO TAKE GOOD CARE OF IT

VIRTUE NUMBER THREE: FORTITUDE

READ ON!

I saw Nelson Mandela at very close proximity In December 1993 in Johannesburg when he came to address the African Methodist Episcopal church annual conference. He was a very tall and slender gentleman but was visibly full of confidence. In his address he referred to his famous *"I am prepared to die"* speech and this is an embodiment of what fortitude is all about-the ability to be bold and stand for the truth regardless. This speech is so titled because it ends with the words: *"It is an ideal for which I am prepared to die"*. He delivered this three hour speech from the dock (Rivonia Trial) in Pretoria on 20 April 1964.The synopsis of his speech read as follows:

"During my lifetime I have dedicated my life to the struggle of the African people. I have fought against White domination and I have against Black domination. I have cherished the ideal of a democratic and free society in which all people will live together in harmony and with equal opportunities. It is the ideal for which I hope to live for and to see realised. But, my Lord, if need be, it is an ideal for which I am prepared to die". (From Wikipedia, 04-03-2019)

- *The "I am prepared to die"* sentence was used by South African composer Michael Hankinson in his 2004 orchestra work *"A Mandela Portrait"* as the choral finale of the first movement.

- The last paragraph of the speech is written on the wall of South Africa's Constitutional Court building in Johannesburg.

- USA President Barak Obama quoted from this speech during his tribute speech at the state memorial service for Nelson Mandela on 10 December 2013.

I was a Grade Three rural learner when Nelson Mandela and his fellow comrades received life sentences in April 1964.They were all sent to the notorious Robben Island prison to serve their life sentences. I was still too young to understand all these but later I began to appreciate what these developments meant for us. The South African government never allowed us to see his photo or to read about him. All seemed doom and gloom. But 27 years thereafter everything became rosy again. He became the first democratically elected black president of South Africa in April 1994.The fortitude virtue he displayed in 1964 was still the same when he was ultimately released from prison. Nelson Mandela was born on the 18th of July 1919 in Mveso village-Eastern Cape. Born to the abaThembu nation, Nelson Mandela's quest for freedom was to consist of a painful and yet courageous journey. This included imprisonment which also led to his poor health which would affect him greatly later in life. Intending to gain skills needed to become a privy counsellor for the Thembu royal house decided to go through primary, secondary and even university education.

Every year on 18 July-the day Nelson Mandela was born-the UN joins the whole world in devoting 67 minutes to worthy human services. Every time I visit Pretoria church square-and look at the Palace of Justice building across the square, my mind goes back to what took place there many years ago. The famous Rivonia Trial took place there. The building forms part of the northern façade of the square and dates back to 8-06-1897 when the foundation stone was laid by President Paul Kruger. Palace of Justice is currently the headquarters of the Gauteng Division of High Court of South Africa

WHAT IS FORTITUDE?

Read the following statement. Peter and John spoke right back and said: *"Whether it's right in God's eyes to listen to you rather than to God, you decide. As for us there is no question-we can't keep quiet about what we've seen and heard"*. (Acts 4:19-20).We sometimes become afraid to share our faith because people might feel uncomfortable and might reject us. We just lack courage to stand for the truth. But Peter and John's zeal for the Lord was so strong that they could not keep quite even when threatened. This is the essence of fortitude. We need to be bold in all we say and do. If your courage to witness for God or stand for the truth has weakened, pray that your boldness may increase again. Fortitude is a very important virtue and all humans should strive to acquire it. Fortitude means to display courage in pain or in adversity. Other words describing fortitude are: Daring, bravery, guts, boldness, backbone and strength. Fortitude enables you to do, stand or defend what is right in the face of difficulties. We cannot deny the fact that making life or death decisions is always a challenge but we cannot run away from such a heavy responsibility. We have to say "yes" or "no" even though this is sometimes a very difficult and a dicey challenge. But fortitude always help us to succeed. It always carries us through the storms of life and makes us to succeed against all odds.

PAUL: MAN OF FORTITUDE

Paul means "little". Little as he may have been, no person apart from Christ himself, shaped the history of Christianity like the Apostle Paul. Even before he was a believer, his actions were significant. His frenzied persecution of Christians following Stephen's death got the church started in obeying Christ's final command to take the Gospel worldwide. Paul's personal encounter with Christ changed his life. He never lost his fierce intensity, but from then on it was channelled for the Gospel. He was very religious. His training under Gamaliel was the finest available. His intentions and efforts were sincere. He was a good Pharisee, who knew the Bible and sincerely believed that the Christian movement was dangerous to Judaism. Thus he hated Christians and persecuted them without mercy. He was very bold and very forthright-a man of fortitude through and through……

He set out to destroy Christianity by persecuting Christians. But God stopped him in his hurried tracks on the Damascus road. He personally met Jesus Christ, and his life was never again. God did not waste any Part of Paul-his background, his training, his citizenship, his mind, his courage or even his weaknesses. (1) He witnessed for Jesus Christ throughout the Roman Empire on three missionary journeys. (11) He wrote (13) letters to various churches, which became part of the New Testament. (111) He was never afraid to face an issue head-on and deal with it precisely.(1v) He was sensitive to God's leading and, despite his strong personality, always did as God directed.(v) He is often called the Apostle to the Gentiles. He was born in Tarsus but he became a world traveller for Jesus Christ. He summed up his life's vision and mission as follows: *"For me to live be Christ and to die is gain. If I am to go on living in the body, this will mean fruitful labour for me, yet what shall I choose? I do not know! I am torn between the two; I desire to depart and be with Jesus Christ, which is better by far, but it is more necessary for you that I remain in the body"*. (Philippians 1:21-24).He concluded his life of fortitude episode when he wrote to young Timothy and said: *"I have fought a good fight. I have finished the race. I have kept the faith. Now there is in store for me the crown of righteousness which the Lord, the righteous judge, will award it to me on that day"*. (2 Tim.4:7-8). Paul story is told in (Acts 7:58-28:31) and throughout his New Testament letters

LIFE-SKILLS LESSONS

We may draw the following life-skills lessons from this very important third virtue. These are:

- Fortitude is the strength of character that enables you to endure pain or adversity with courage. The word often used in the Bible for fortitude is endurance, strength or perseverance. Not only is fortitude a great quality, but we are commanded to pursue it. Paul encouraged Timothy in this regard and said: *"Endure hardship with us like a good soldier of Jesus Christ"*. Like soldiers, we have to give up worldly security and endure rigorous discipline. Like athletes, we must train hard and follow the rules. And like farmers, we must work extremely hard and be patient. They do not know when the rain is going to fall but they work hard all round to make sure that they produce good harvest.

- Fortitude helps you to stand firm against persecution. In the days when the books of the New Testament were being penned, persecution against Christians was escalating (Acts 8:1).To is a follower of Jesus Christ could mean the loss of property, position and even life. So the Apostles and leaders continually urged the budding new churches to stand strong, have courage and endure for the sake of Jesus Christ. We are also encouraged nowadays to endure, develop fortitude and grow in our faith and character and be more like Jesus Christ. Fortitude is not needed on sunny days on the beach. It is needed in the storm of life.

- We develop fortitude as we walk with Jesus Christ, following His commands, refusing to turn to the left or to the right and letting His Word be the lamp to our feet and the light to our path. (Psalm 119:105).When we have persevered and overcome this world, the Lord promises us that we will reign with Him forever.(Revelation 2:26;3:21).Fortitude is possible through the power of the Holy Spirit only (Luke 12:11) and is rewarded by our Father in heaven. God is always faithful and will surely reward those who are faithful to him and observe his commandments.

- One enemy of fortitude is the incorrect assumption that we know how things will end. When a situation seems out of control or does not appear to be headed in the right direction, we tend to write "The end" over the story. We think we know the final result, so, instead of exercising fortitude, we give up or take matters into our own hands.(Proverbs 35:6) is a good passage to cling to whenever we can see only disaster: *"Trust in the Lord with all your heart, and lean not to your own understanding. In all your ways acknowledge him, and he shall direct your paths"*.

SELF-ASSESSMENT ON FORTITUDE

GIFTING	LOW	AVERAGE	GOOD
• My courage skill is?			
• My bravery skill is?			
• My daring skill is?			
• My boldness skill is?			
• My will-power skill is?			

ACTIONS POINTS

I will improve and maintain my fortitude by:

1.	
2.	
3.	
4.	
5.	

DAILY SCRIPTURES ON: THE BENEFITS OF FORTITUDE

(To inspire and guide you as you go about your daily business)

DAY 1:*"Do not swerve to the right or to the left; keep your foot from evil"*. (Proverbs 4:27).

DAY 2:*"let us hold unswervingly to the hope we profess, for he who promised is faithful"*. *(*Hebrews 10:23)

DAY 3:*"See that what you have heard from the beginning remains in you. If it does, you will remain in the Son and in the Father"*. (1 John 2:24).

DAY 4:*"Keep your head in all situations, endure hardship, do the work of an evangelist, discharge all the duties of your ministry"*. (2 Timothy 4:5).

DAY 5:*"Whenever happens, conduct yourselves in a manner worthy of the Gospel of Christ .Then, whether I come and see you or only hear about you in my absence, I will know that you stand firm in one spirit, contending as one man for the faith of the Gospel".(Philippians 1:27).*

DAY 6:*"Search me, O God and know my heart; test me and know my anxious thoughts. See if there is any offensive way in me, and lead me in the way everlasting"*. (Psalm 138:23-24).

DAY 7:*"May the God who gives endurance and encouragement, give you a spirit of unity among yourselves as you follow Christ Jesus so that with one heart and mouth you may glorify the God and Father of our Lord Jesus Christ"*. (Romans 15:5-6).

SELF-CONTROL

GENERAL FEATURES

Self-disciple

Self-denial

Will-power

Self-possession

Self-determination

THE VIRTUE OF SELF-CONTROL BLOSSOM LIKE A
FLOWER WHEN PROPERLY NURTURED

SO! MAKE A DECISION TODAY TO TAKE GOOD CARE OF IT

VIRTUE NUMBER FOUR: SELF-CONTROL

READ ON!

I arrived at White River Southern Sun hotel one Sunday afternoon in 1995.The purpose of my trip was to conduct a week long Freelance Marketers training course. We invited 40 different marketers from the different regions of the beautiful Mpumalanga province. White River is about 267km. from Polokwane and I knew for sure that I was going to face a very tough and challenging week away from my family. But I was well prepared and very much equal to the task. We started our training on Monday morning and everything went on very smoothly until Thursday during lunch time. I decided to go to my room and rest for an hour. I tried to open my door but my card did not function properly. I struggled for a while but still could not succeed. I saw three hotel women cleaners resting under a tree and I beckoned them for help. They do have master cards to open all the doors after all. One young lady came rushing and used her master card to open my door. I thanked her for her help and stepped inside. She followed me into my room and made herself comfortable on one of my chairs.

"What is happening now? "I asked.

I cleaned your room since Monday and I observed that you have spent four nights alone. I have decided to become your companion tonight. I will arrive at 11h00 when I knock off". She left my room before I could respond.

I did not worry much because I am a man of strong self-control and I know what to do under such devil invested circumstances. I went for my afternoon session, then for my diner and thereafter straight to my room with a clear plan in mind. The first plan was to use my shooter and lock myself in until the next morning. But then it meant that I will not venture out of my room until the next day. To my uttermost disgust I found that my door shooter was broken and the time was already approaching 20h30.I had to come up with a quick plan to safe guard myself. I sat on my bed and started praying for a solution. A sudden idea which I believe came from God struck my mind.

"You brought along three beautiful set ties from Polokwane for this trip, didn't you? "Yes I did!"

Take one of your beautiful ties and tie your toiled door and the main door together.

That will stop this evil woman all together with her evil intensions".

I did exactly as I was instructed and I went into a deep peaceful sleep. I do not know up to this day whether she came to my room at 20h30 because I slept like a baby that evening. I woke up the following morning so refreshed as if I did not have serious challenges the previous night. The good news was that, that Friday was my last day at White River sun. All I had to do was to go for my morning breakfast and drive to home. Guess what I discovered when I sat at the table to enjoy my breakfast? The very same evil lady who nearly brought down my hard earned integrity I inculcated into my character for so many was there to serve me. She was so angry and was just forcing herself to serve me. I did not take an offence though because I understood the ugly politics she put herself into the previous night. I went home in one piece and my self-control won the day.

WHAT IS SELF-CONTROL

Self-control is the fourth essential virtue all humans should strive to possess. Self-control means the power of controlling one's external reactions, and emotions. It is our God given ability to help us to govern ourselves. It is our God given ability to regulate our emotions, thoughts and behaviour in the face of temptations and impulses and help us to achieve specific goals. Other words describing self-control are: Self-discipline, self-denial, will-power, restraint, self-possession and determination. It enables us to control our temper, regulate our sensual appetite and possessions. It even enables us to pursue legitimate pleasures in moderation. It enables us to wait and to delay our self-gratification so that we can later achieve our higher and distant goals. Everything will fall into place once you have developed a full sense of self-control.

It is the quality that allows you to stop yourself from doing things you want to do that might not be in your best interest. For example, without self-control you might burp and curse non-stop. Not charging expensive things you want to a credit card takes self-control. Getting up early for work takes self-control. Without self-control, it is hard to get far in life. Self-control is similar to self-discipline. Self-control is primarily rooted in your pre-frontal cortex, which is significantly larger in humans than in animals. Thanks to the pre-frontal cortex, because it immediately responds to every impulse as it arises. Through self-control, individuals can plan, evaluate alternative actions, and ideally avoid things they'll later regret. The ability to exert self-control is typically called willpower. Willpower allows you to direct your attention, and it underlines all kinds of your achievements, from school to workplace. When you master yourself appropriately, the whole world opens up for you.

REASONS FOR SELF-CONTROL

- Self-control helps us to control our anger. People with good patience do well in life than people with bad tempers. King Solomon expressed this factor very clearly when he said, *"Better a patient man than a warrior, a man who controls his temper than the one who takes a city"* (Proverbs 16:32). Patience is the direct opposite of anger and is the fruit of the spirit. Patience always drives away anger and there is no law in the whole world that can prevail against it. So! We better develop a superior self-control quality in our lives.

- Self-control helps us to express our positivity. Simon Peter summed up the importance of self-control when he said. *"For this reason, make every effort to add to your faith goodness and to goodness, knowledge and to knowledge self-control, and to self-control, perseverance, and to perseverance, godliness, and to godliness, brotherly kindness and to brotherly kindness, love"*. (2 Peter 1:5-7)

- Self-control helps us to control sexual sins. Sexual sins are real challenges and they have brought many people around the world down on their knees. Paul shared a light to the Thessalonian church when he said, *"It is God's will that you should be sanctified: that you should avoid sexual immorality. That each of you should learn to control his own body, in a way that is holy and honourable"*. (1 Thessalonians 3-5). Sexual sins are always challenging us to the limit and we need self-control to overcome those challenges. Many saints before us, and Joseph (Genesis 39:11-23) being one of them. Potiphar's wife caught him by his cloak and said, *"Come to bed with me but he left his cloak in her hand and ran out of the house"*.

- Self-control helps us to prepare for Christ's return. One factor that is definitely clear all over the world today is the fact that this world is going to come to an end. This fact is very clear.

Paul encourages all of us to prepare for Jesus Christ's return when he wrote to the Thessalonian church and said, *"So then, let us not be like others, who are asleep, but let us be alert and self-controlled. For those who sleep, sleeps at night, and those who get drunk, get drunk at night. But since we belong to the day, let us be self-controlled, putting on faith and love as breastplate and the hope of salvation as helmet".*(1 Thessalonians 5:6-8)

- Self-control enables us to pray properly. Simon Peter alluded to this important prayer factor when he said, *"The end of all things is near. Therefore be clearing minded and self-controlled so that you can pray".* (1 Peter 4:7).One important factor that eludes many Christians is the ability to stay focused in their faith and to prepare adequately for the second coming of our Lord Jesus Christ. The story of the ten virgins (Matthew25:1-13) is a perfect example in this regard. And self-control helps us to pray properly without losing direction along the way.

- Self-control helps us to show our resistance to the devil. The evil one is our number one enemy and good self-control helps us to keep him in his place. Simon Peter highlighted this factor when he said. *"Be self-controlled and alert. Your enemy the devil prowls around like a roaring lion looking for someone to devour".* (1 Peter 5:8).The devil operates like a lion. It attacks sick, young or struggling animals. They choose victims who are alone or not alert. We should watch out for Satan when we are suffering or being persecuted. He attack us when we are at our lowest ebb. When we are sick or facing tremendous life's challenges.

SAMUEL: MAN OF SELF-CONTROL

Samuel was an embodiment of self-control and he displayed this virtue loud and clear throughout his life. From his youth, he aided the high priest Eli in the shrine at Shiloh. In his farewell speech, he asked the Israelites to point out any wrongs he might have committed during his time as Israel's judge. He said, *"Here I stand. Testify against me I the presence of the Lord and his anointed. Whose ox have I taken? Whose donkey have I taken? Who have I cheated? Who have I oppressed? From whose hand have I accepted a bribe to make me shut my eyes? If I have done any of these, I will make right. You have not cheated or oppressed us"* (1 Samuel 12:1-4).By doing so, he was reminding them that he could be trusted to tell the truth. He judged Israel well throughout his life. He saved them from the Philistines and led them back to God.

The name Samuel comes from the Hebrew expression, "heard of God" and God shaped him from the start. Samuel was probably three years old-the customary age of weaning (1 Samuel 1:28)-when his mother left him at the tabernacle. By saying, *"I give him to the Lord,* "Hannah meant that she was dedicating Samuel to God for the life-time service. She did not, of course forget her much wanted son. She visited him regularly. And each year she brought him a robe just like Eli's (1 Samuel 21:9-20).In later years, Samuel lived in Ramah (1 Samuel 7:17), his parents' hometown (1 Sal 1:19-20) here he headed groups of prophets devoted to the restoration of the traditional worship. Like Moses, Samuel was called to fill many different roles: Judge, priest, prophet, counsellor and God's man at the turning point of Israel. God worked through Samuel because Samuel was willing to be one thing: God's servant. He was responsible for the establishment of the monarchy

Samuel moved ahead because he was listening to God's direction. *"The Lord was with him as he grew up, and let none of his words fall to the ground. And all Israel from Dan to Beersheba recognised that Samuel was attested as a prophet of the Lord"* (1 Samuel 3:19-20).His obedience and dedication to God made him one of the greatest judges In Israel's history. Too often we ask God to control our lives without making us give up the goals for which we strive. We ask God to help us get where we want to go but we often fail because of lack self-control. The first step in correcting this tendency is to turn over both the control and destination of our lives to him. The second step is to be to do what we already know God requires of us. The third step is to listen for further direction from his word. Samuel story is told In (1 Samuel 1-28).He is also mentioned in (Psalm 99:6,Jeremiah 15:1,Acts 3:24, 13:20 and Hebrews 11:32).

SELF-ASSESSMENT ON SELF-CONTROL

GIFTING	LOW	AVERAGE	GOOD
• My self-discipline skill is?			
• My self-denial skill is?			
• My will-power skill is?			
• My self-possession skill is?			
• My self-determination skill is?			

ACTION POINTS

I will improve and maintain my self-control by:

1.	
2.	
3.	
4.	
5.	

DAILY SCRIPTURE ON: BENEFITS OF SELF-CONTROL

(To inspire and guide you as you go about your daily business)

DAY 1: *"He who guards his lips guards his life, but he who speaks rashly will come to ruin". (*Proverbs 13:3).

DAY 2:*"Let those who love hate evil, for he guards the lives of his faithful ones".* (Psalm 97:10)

DAY 3:*"Live by the spirit, and you will not gratify the desires of the sinful nature".* (Galatians 5:16)

DAY 4:*"Whatever happens, conduct yourself in a manner worthy of the Gospel of Christ. Then whether I come and see you or only hear about you in my absence, I will know that you stand firm in one spirit, contenting as one man for the faith of the Gospel".* (Philippians 1:27)

DAY 5: *"Make it your ambition to lead a quiet life, to mind your own business and to work with your own hands, just as we told you so that your daily life may win the respect of outsiders and so that you will not be dependent on anybody"* (1 Thessalonians 4:11-12).

DAY 6. *"Do not be overcome by evil, but overcome evil with good". (Romans 12:21)*

DAY 7:*"The name of the Lord is a strong tower, the righteous run to it are safe".* (Proverbs 18:10)

VIRTUE NUMBER FIVE:

LOVE

GENERAL FEATURES

Friendship

Affection

Attachment

Fondness

Adoration

THE VIRTUE OF LOVE BLOSSOM LIKE A FLOWER WHEN PROPERLY NURTURED.

SO! MAKE A DECISION TODAY TO TAKE GOOD CARE OF IT

VIRTUE NUMBER FIVE: LOVE

READ ON!

Mary Teresa Bojaxhiu commonly called Mother Teresa was an embodiment of love. She was born Agnes Gonxha Bojaxhiu in Skopje, Macedonia on 20 August 1910.Her family was Albanian descendants. At the age of 12 she felt strongly the call of God. She knew she had to become a missionary to spread the love of Jesus Christ. At the age of 18 she left her parental home in Skopje and joined Sisters of Loreto-an Irish Community of Nuns with a mission to India. After a few months training in Dublin, she was sent to India where on 24 May 1931 she took her initial vows as a Nun. From 1931-1948, Mother Teresa taught at St. Mary's High School in Calcutta. But the suffering and poverty she glimpsed outside the convent walls made such deep impression on her so much so that in 1948 she applied and received permission from her supervisors to leave the convent school and devote herself to working among the poorest of the poor in the slums of Calcutta.

Although she had no funds, she depended on Divine Provision and started an open air school for slum children. Soon she was joined by voluntary helpers and financial support was also forthcoming. This aid made it possible for her to extend the scope of her work and serve many more children. Today the Order comprises of active and comprehensive branches of Sisters and Brothers in many countries. In 1963 both the Comparative branch of Sisters and the active branches of Brothers was founded. In 1979 the Comparative branch of Brothers was added and in 1984 Priests branch was established. The society of Missionaries Mother Teresa established many years ago has spread all over the world. It is still driven by the same old fundamental principle *"Love God with all your heart and love your fellowman as you loves yourself"*. It is found in the Former Soviet Union and in Eastern Europe countries. They provide effective help to the poorest of the poor in Asia, Africa and Latin America. Mother Teresa won the Nobel Peace Prize in 1979.She died on 5 September 1997.She was canonized on 4 September 2016 at Saint Peter's square, Vatican City by Pope Francis.

WHAT IS LOVE

Consider the following statement*: "Love the Lord your God with all your passion and prayer and intelligence. This is the most important virtue and the first on any list. But there is a second to set alongside it: Love others as well as you love yourself. These two commands are pegs; everything in God's law and the prophets hangs from it). (Matthew 22:37-40):* By Eugene H. Peterson. Love is the fifth essential virtue all humans should strive for and possess. Love means a great liking. Love is our willingness to sacrifice for the sake of another person. Love enables us to love ourselves and our neighbour. Love goes beyond justice it demands from us to deliver more than what fairness requires. It requires us to love even our strangers and do well to all humans It challenges us to love even our enemies. A whole cluster of important human virtues such as, empathy, compassion, kindness, generosity, service and loyalty all make up the virtue of love. Paul emphasised the importance of love when he wrote to the Corinthians church and said, *"If I speak in the tongues of men and of angels, but have no love, I am only a resounding gong or a clanging cymbal. If I have the gift of prophesy and can fathom all mysteries and all knowledge... then I am nothing"*. (1 Corinthians 13:1)

RUTH & NAOMI: WOMEN OF LOVE

Ruth "friend "and Naomi "Gracious or pleasant" are true examples of the virtue of love. Ruth was a Moabite and Naomi an Israelite. But their lives were so closely woven together so closely that they were almost inseparable. Ruth loved her mother-in-law dearly. They are good examples of real love. Their cultures, family backgrounds, and ages were very different. As mother-in-law and daughter-in-law, they probably had as many opportunities for tension as for tenderness. And yet they were bound to each other. As a result, Ruth became the great-grandmother of David and an ancestor in the line of Jesus Christ the Messiah. What a profound impact Naomi's life made!

Ruth and Naomi shared deep sorrow, great affection for each other and an overriding commitment to the God of Israel. And yet as much as they depended on each other, they also gave each other space and freedom in their commitment to one another. Naomi was willing to let Ruth return to her family but Ruth was willing to leave her homeland and go and live in Israel. Recently widowed, Ruth begged to stay with Naomi wherever she went, even though it would mean leaving her homeland: *"Your people will be my people and your God my God"* (Ruth 1:16).God was at the centre of their intimate love. Ruth came to know God of Israel through Naomi. The older woman allowed Ruth to see, hear and feel all the joy and anguish of her relationship God.

No matter how discouraging or antagonistic the world may seem, love will always prevail. There are people out there who follow God and love their fellow man. God will use anyone who is open to him to achieve his purposes. As Naomi discovered, when you act selflessly, others are encouraged to follow your example. Ruth was a Moabites and Boaz was a descendant of Rahab, a former prostitute from Jericho (Joshua 6:22-23).Nevertheless their offspring continued the family line through which Jesus Christ came into the world (Matthew 1:5-6).

LIFE-SKILLS LESSONS

We may draw the following life-skills from this important fifth virtue. These are:

- We must remain in love always. You will do well in your Christian walk if you can observe this important fundamental principle. Otherwise you will lose out and be cast out. Jesus Christ taught his disciples and said. *"As the father has loved me, so I have loved you. Now remain in my love. If you obey my commands, you will remain in my love, just as I have obeyed my father's commands and remain in his love"*.(John 15 9-10)

- Love motivates us to love others. It encourages us to love our fellow human beings as we love ourselves. Jesus Christ encouraged his disciples in this regard and said, (Jon 13:34-35) *"A new commandment I give unto you; love one another. As I have loved you (, so you must love one another. By this all men will know that you are my disciples if you love one another*

- We must be directed into it. We should always take concerted efforts to make sure we practice love in all we do. In our personal lives, family, career and in our social responsibilities. Paul shared this aspect of love with the Thessalonian church and said, *"We are not looking for praise from men, not from you or anyone else…We love you so much that we delighted to share with you not only gospel of God but our lives as well, because you have become so dear to us"*. (2 Thessalonians 2:6-8)

- We must keep ourselves in it. Losing God's love is something a very simple act to do even though we know that God will never live us or forsake us. We lose God's love because of the wrong choices we make. Jude wrote to the diaspora Jewish church and said, *"Keep yourselves in God's love as you wait for the mercy of our Lord Jesus Christ to bring you to eternal life. Be merciful to those who doubt".* *(Jude 21-22)*

- Love is everlasting. God's love for us does not have an end. God declared to Israel through Jeremiah and said, *"I have loved you with an everlasting love; I have drawn you with loving-kindness"* (Jeremiah 31:3).The only dead end we can ever reach in is by rejecting him completely and taking him totally out of our lives.

SELF-ASSESSMENT ON LOVE

GIFTING	LOW	AVERAGE	GOOD
• My friendship skill is?			
• My affection skill is?			
• My attachment skill is?			
• My fondness skill is?			
• My adoration skill is			

ACTION POINTS

I will improve and maintain love by:

1.	
2.	
3.	
4.	
5.	

DAILY SCRIPTURES: ON THE BENEFITS OF LOVE

To inspire and guide you as you go about your daily business:

- DAY 1: And *he has given us this command. Whoever loves God must also love his brother".* *(1 John 4:21)*

- DAY 2:*"My command is this; love each other as I have loved you. Greater love has no one than this that he lay down his life for his friends".* (John 15:12-13)

- DAY 3: *"You my brothers, were called to be free. But do not use your freedom to indulge the sinful nature, rather serve one another in love Galatians 5:13*

- *DAY 4: "Keep on loving each other as brothers. Do not forget to entertain strangers, for by so doing some people has entertained angels without knowing it".* (Hebrews 13:1-2)

- DAY 5:*"Now that you have purified yourself by obeying the truth so that you have sincere love for your brothers, love one another deeply from the heart".*(1 Peter 1:22)

- DAY 6:*"And now dear lady, I am not writing you a new command but the one we had from the beginning. I ask that we love one another. And this is love that we walk in obedience to his command".* (2 John 5-6)

- DAY 7:*"And this is my prayer; that your love may abound more and more in knowledge and depth and depth of insight so that you may be able to discern what is best and may be pure and blameless until the day of Christ".*(Phil 1:9-10)

POSITIVE ATTITUDE

GENERAL FEATURES

Positive faith

Mental goodness

Positive mind set

Positive thinking

Positive disposition

THE VIRTUE OF POSITIVE ATTITUDE BLOSSOM LIKE
A FLOWER WHEN NURTURED PROPERLY

SO! MAKE A DECISION TODAY TO TAKE GOOD CARE OF IT

VIRTUE NUMBER SIX: POSITIVE ATTITUDE

READ ON!

Nicholas James Vujicic is an embodiment of positive attitude. Amazing Nick Vujicic was born with no arms or legs. He was born with a rare disease called *tetra-Amelia syndrome*. He was born in 1982 in Mebourne-Australia. His three sonograms failed to reveal his complications, and yet the Vujicic family were destined to cope with both challenges of raising a son who refused to allow his physical condition to limit his lifestyle. He is an evangelist, philanthropist and a motivational speaker. His bestsellers, "Life without limps, Unstoppable and Stand strong" are some of the books he penned. He is married to his beautiful wife Kanae Miyahara and is blessed with four children. He holds a Baccalaureate degree. In January 2007 Nick and family made long journey from Australia to Southern California-USA where he is the President of the international non-profit ministry "Life without limbs" which was established in 2005. His organisation is worth $500 million today.

The early days were very difficult. Throughout his childhood, Nick not only dealt with typical challenges of school but he also struggled with depression and loneliness. But his positive attitude towards life pulled him through. He constantly wondered why he was different than all other kids around him. He also questioned the purpose of his life or if he even had a purpose at all. According to him, the victory over his struggle as well as his strength and passion for life today, can be accredited to his faith in God, his family and friends and many more people who have inspired him to carry on. Since his first speaking engagement at the age of 19 Nick has travelled around the world sharing his story with millions, sometimes in stadiums filled to capacity, speaking to diverse groups such as students, teachers, young people, business professionals and church congregations of all sizes.

Today this young evangelist has accomplished more than most people achieve in a lifetime. He is an author, musician and actor. His hobbies include fishing, painting and swimming. He says, "*If God can* use a man without arms and legs to be his hands and feet, then he will certainly use any willing *heart*". His latest foray into radio will expand his platform for inviting men and women all around the world to embrace hope and message of Jesus Christ. He is a real marvel to watch.

WHAT IS A POSITIVE ATTITUDE

Positive attitude is the sixth essential virtue humans should strive for and possess. Positive means "to be sure or to be certain". Attitude means a position, opinion, feeling or a point of view. Positive attitude therefore means a sure or a certain point of view. If you have a positive attitude, you become an asset to yourself. But if you have a negative attitude, you become a burden to yourself and others. Positive attitude is characterised by good character traits such as hope, enthusiasm, flexibility and sense of humour. All of us need to be reminded that we have the ability to choose a positive attitude instead of a negative attitude.

King Solomon highlighted the importance of positive attitude when he said, "*Two things I ask of you O lord; do not refuse me before I die. Keep falsehood and lies far from me; give me neither poverty nor riches, but give me only my daily bread. Otherwise, I may have too much and disown you and say 'who is the Lord? 'Or I may become poor and steal and so dishonour the name of God*" (Pro.30:7-9).

BARNABAS: MAN OF POSITIVE ATTITUDE

The name Barnabas means "Son of Encouragement". He displayed positive attitude throughout his life. He was a native of Cyprus and member of Jerusalem church. He sold his land to give money to the poor Christians in Judea. Every group needs an "encourager" because everyone needs encouragement at one time or another. A man named Joseph was such an encourager that he earned nickname Son of Encouragement or Barnabas, from the Jerusalem church. He was always drawn to people he could encourage, and he was a great help to those around him. It is delightful that whenever Barnabas encouraged Christians, non-Christians flocked to become believers too. His actions were very crucial to the early church. He sold his property and shares the profits with the early church. God used his relationship with Paul at one point and with John Mark at another to keep these two men going when either might have failed. He did wonders with positive attitude and encouragement.

When Paul arrived in Jerusalem for the first time following his conversion, the local Christians were understandably reluctant to welcome him. They thought his story was a trick to capture more Christians. Only Barnabas proved willing to risk his life to meet with Paul and then convinced others that their former enemy was now a vibrant believer in Jesus Christ. We can only wonder what might have happened to Paul without Barnabas. It was Barnabas who encouraged John Mark to go with him and Paul to Antioch. John Mark joined them on their first missionary journey but decided during the trip to return home. Later Barnabas wanted to invite John Mark to join them for another journey but Paul would not agree. As a result, the partners went their separate ways.Barnabas with John and Paul with Silas. But Barnabas remains true to his character regardless. He was the encourager through and through. He never lost sight of his life's vision and mission. He carried on doing a good job

Barnabas's patient positive attitude and encouragement was confirmed by John Mark's eventual ministry. Paul and John Mark were later reunited in missionary efforts. As Barnabas shows, we are rarely in a situation where there isn't someone we can encourage. Our tendency, however is to criticise instead. It may be important at times to point out someone's shortcomings, but before we have the right to do this, we must build that person's trust through encouragement. However the value of encouragement is often missed because it turns to be private rather than public. Are you prepared to encourage those with whom you come in contact today? Barnabas story is told in Acts (4:36, 37; 9:27-15:39). He is also mentioned in (1 Cor. 9:6, Gal. 2:1, 9, 13 and Col. 4:10)

LIFE-SKILLS LESSONS

We may draw the following life-skills lessons from this important virtue:

- Positive attitude is a state of mind that envisions and expects positive results. Positive attitude helps us to live a purpose driven life. It helps us to set measurable and achievable goals. You live a life of meaning and you are able to achieve your goals.

- Positive attitude is the willingness to try doing new things. Positive attitude helps us to live a life out of a box. It helps us to visualise and try new things. It helps us to see beyond our present circumstances and cultivate a will to overcome those circumstances.

- Positive attitude is a belief that everything would turn all right. It is a belief that always sees a "Utopia" in the main frame of God's creation. It is an attitude that helps us to see the brighter sight of life instead of seeing doom and gloom only.

- It is an attitude that says to us: "*When you see darkness, do not lose hope because sunshine is just around the corner* "It is an attitude that helps us to see thc good in people. Positive attitude helps us to discern and develop the God given "Good" in every person because every human being is born with a certain amount of good hidden right inside his heart. This is the hidden treasure that needs to be unearthed and positive attitude is able to reach such depth lying hidden and bring them to the surface.

- Positive attitude is a mental attitude that sees the good and the accomplishments in your life rather than negatives and failures. Every human being is born with gifts and talents. Gifts and talents are always good and perfect. God endowed us with these gifts and talents so that we can uplift ourselves and our societies. Positive attitude help us to discover these gifts and talents and pursue them until we reach our goals.

- Positive attitude is a mind-set that helps you to see and recognise opportunities. We are living in the world of opportunities. Wherever we try to turn to there are opportunities. There are opportunities at every door we knock at. There opportunities around every corner. If it was not so, then the world would have come to an end. Positive attitude is the main sources that helps us to smell, see, touch and taste these opportunities, seize them and own them. Psychologists inform us that our brains are as big as our clinched fists and are full of creative ideas. But we are only informed that we only use half of our mental capabilities until God calls us home. We just do not possess enough mental attitudes.

- Positive attitude is an attitude that helps you to improve your self-esteem. It helps you to develop your positive self-confidence. That is, to have confidence in your own worth, abilities or self-respect. It encompasses beliefs about yourself as well as your emotional state such as triumph, despair, pride and shame.

SELF-ASSESSMENT ON POSITIVE ATTITUDE

GIFTING	LOW	AVERAGE	GOOD
• My positive faith skill is?			
• Mental goodness skill is?			
• My positive mind set skill is?			
• My positive thinking skill is?			
• My positive disposition skill is?			

ACTIONS POINTS

I will improve and maintain positive attitude by:

1.	
2.	
3.	
4.	
5.	

DAILY SCRIPTURES ON: BENEFITS OF POSITIVE ATTITUDE

(To inspire and guide you as you go about your daily business)

DAY 1:*"You love righteousness and hate wickedness; therefore God, your God, has set you above your companions by anointing you with the oil of joy"* (Psalm 45:7).

DAY 2: *"But seek first his kingdom and his righteousness and all these things will be given to you as well. Therefore does not worry about tomorrow for tomorrow will worry about itself? Each day has enough troubles of its own".* (Matthew 7:33-34)

DAY 3:*"Whatever is true, whatever is noble, whatever is right, whatever is pure, whatever is lovely, whatever is admirable-if anything is excellent or praiseworthy-think about such things".*

DAY 4: *"Speak to one another with psalms, hymns and spiritual songs, sing and make music in your heart to the Lord always giving thanks to God the Father for everything in the name of our Lord Jesus Christ".* (Ephesians 5:19-20)

DAY 5:*"You are already clean because of the word I have spoken to you. Remain in me, and I will remain in you. No branch can bear fruit by itself; it must remain in the wine. Neither can you bear fruit unless you remain in me".* (John 15:3-4)

DAY 6:*"Do not worry about what your life, what you will eat; or about your body, what you will wear. Life is more than food and the body more than clothes".* (Luke 12:22-23)

DAY 7: *"So do not throw away your confidence; it will be richly rewarded. You need to persevere so that when you have done the will of God, you will receive what he has promised".* (He. 10:35-36)

VIRTUE NUMBER SEVEN:

HARD-WORKING

GENERAL FEATURES

Diligence

Industrious

Perseverance

Painstaking

Untiring

THE VIRTUE OF HARD-WORKING BLOSSOM LIKE A
FLOWER WHEN NURTURED PROPERLY.

SO! MAKE A DECISION TODAY TO TAKE GOOD CARE OF IT.

VIRTUE NUMBER SEVEN: HARD-WORKING

READ ON

Aquila and Priscilla was a hard-working couple. They complemented each other, capitalize on each other's strengths and form an effective team. They are never mentioned separately in the Bible. They earned their living by making tents and were very successful at their art. Aquila which means 'Eagle' was a godly Jewish Christian, husband of Priscilla and friend and faithful supporter of Paul. Aquila was born in Pontus but later decided to establish their tent making business in Rome with her wife. They were unfortunately expelled from Rome by Emperor Claudius together with the other Jews. Priscilla who means 'Ancient one' was Aquila's wife. Her name comes before Aquila and from this it has been concluded that Priscilla was very exceptional in some way. She was very talented and was a hard-working woman. Six or seven times Pricilla and Aquila are mentioned in the NT.

Priscilla and Aquila met Paul in Corinth during his second missionary journey. They had just been expelled from Rome by Emperor Claudius. Priscilla, Aquila and Paul were tent-makers and Paul worked and stayed with them. Their home was as movable as the tents they made to support themselves. Paul shared with them his wealth of spiritual wisdom. Priscilla and Aquila made the most of their spiritual education, while not neglecting their thriving tent-making business. They listened very carefully to sermons and carefully evaluated what the heard. When they heard Apollos speak, they were impressed by his ability, but soon realised that his information was not complete. Instead of open confrontation, the couple quietly took Apollos home and shared with him what he needed to know. They helped him greatly to come to the fuller understanding of the Gospel.

They went on using their home as a warm place for training and worship. They travelled with Paul to Ephesus. Later, after Emperor Claudius's edict had been revoked, they returned to Rome. In Rome and Ephesus the church met in their homes. Paul greatly valued Priscilla and Aquila, calling them 'fellow-workers in Christ' who risked their lives for him and to whom all the Gentile churches were indebted. In an age when the focus is mostly on what happens between husband and wife, Priscilla and Aquila are an example of what can happen through husband and wife. Their hard-work and effectiveness together speaks volumes about their relationship with each other. Their story is told in Acts 18 They are also mentioned in Romans 16:3-5,1 Corinthians 16:19,2 Timothy 4:19.

WHAT IS HARD-WORKING

Consider the following statement: *"Everyone feels at some point that loss of motivation to keep on working hard due to various reasons. When you are working hard, day in and day out, you feel like you are about to burn out. You feel like throwing in the towel. It is only human to feel like that. But hard work will see you through this challenge"*. Hard-working is the seventh essential virtue humans should possess. Hard-working means a steady and careful application of your mental or physical effort to a purpose. Other words describing hard working are: industrious, focused, and thorough and attentiveness. There is no substitute in life for hard working and hard work has never killed anybody. A hard working person is known by the following qualities: Imitativeness, diligence, goal setting and resourcefulness. God's word makes it very clear that we are instructed to work hard and put our best effort forward.

HARD-WORKING LUKE

Luke-a doctor, a Greek and a Gentile Christian was a hard-working man. His name means a light giver. Doctor Luke was a person of compassion. Although we know few facts of his life, he left a strong impression of himself by what he wrote and did. He had a traveling medical practice as Paul's companion. Since the Gospel was often welcomed with whips and stones, the doctor was undoubtedly seldom without patients. It is even possible that Paul's "thorn in the flesh" was some kind of physical ailment that needed Luke's regular attention. He was a close friend and a companion of Paul. Paul deeply appreciated Luke's skills and faithfulness. He was a dedicated hard working man.

God also made special use of Luke as the historian of the early church. He was a man of science, and as a Greek, he was a man of detail. Repeatedly, his descriptions have been proved accurate. His passion for the facts as he recorded the life of Jesus Christ, the spread of the early church and the lives of Christianity's missionaries gives us dependable sources for the basis of our faith. He wrote his own book as well as the book of Acts and the two books go together. Luke stayed in Philippi while Paul, Silas and Timothy continued on the Egnatian Way to Amphipolis. He accomplished all this while staying out of the spotlight. Perhaps his greatest example is the challenge to greatness even when we are not the centre of attention. His strengths and accomplishments are:

- He was a well-educated and well-trained physician.

- He was a careful and exact historian.

- He was a humble, hardworking, faithful and useful companion of Paul.

- He wrote both the Gospel of Luke and the book of Acts.

Luke includes himself in the "we" sections of (Acts 16-28). He is also mentioned in (Luke 1:3, Acts 1:1,Colossians 4:14,2 Timothy 4:11 and Philemon 24).

LIFE-SKILLS LESSONS

We may draw the following life-skills lessons from this very important seventh virtue: These are:

- GOOD FRUITS: Although you may feel weary from hard work, you will ultimately reap the fruits of your labour. All hard work pays handsomely. This is the Gospel truth and there are thousands and thousands testimonies bearing witness to this truth. This might happen in this life or in the life hereafter, but hard work does finally pay and when it pays, it pays well.

- SKILLS AND TALENTS: Remember to work hard so that you may use your skills and talents to benefit others. Hard work helps you to discover out skills and talents. These are usually innate abilities one cannot easily discover. But through hard work you are able to unearth your hidden talents and skills. What follows thereafter is for you is to apply these talents and skills for the benefit of all human beings.

- WORK ETHICS: Ethics are the moral principles or the rules of conduct. Use your good work ethics as an example for people to follow. Perform your duties and responsibilities in such a way that all who are watching you will praise the God of heaven. In all your work related responsibilities, work as if God is watching. You will then be in a position to please your creator and the people you are serving.

- CAPACITY: God give talents to all his children. God will never give you work you cannot handle. God give you responsibilities according to your potentialities, abilities and skills. Therefore there will be no work you cannot handle and succeed in it as long as you work with God and follow his work plan for your life.

- GOD'S PLAN: Remember that God has a plan for you and your hard work will not be done in vain. God laid out a perfect plan for you before you were born. This plan is not designed to hurt you or destroy your future. It is a plan that makes you to prosper and enjoy a good life. It is a plan designed to make God's people around to prosper and be safe.

- PATIENCE AND PRAYER: Patience and prayer are very essential in our career lives. They sustain us and help us to succeed in whatever we are doing. King Solomon explained this fact perfectly clear when he said. *"A patient man has great understanding but a quick-tempered man displays folly Proverbs 14:29)*.When you feel like giving up, maintain patience and prayer that God will see you through times of low motivation

- WORKING FOR GOD: Remember that you are ultimately working for God rather than working for other people. James explained this fact perfectly clear when he said. *"Blessed is the man who perseveres under trial because when he has stood the test, he will receive the crown of life God has promised to those who love him".(James 1:12)*

SELF-ASSESSMENT ON HARD-WORKING

GIFTING	LOW	AVERAGE	GOOD
• My diligence skill is?			
• My industrious skill is?			
• My perseverance skill is?			
• My painstaking skill is?			
• My untiring skill is?			

ACTIONS POINTS

I will improve and maintain my hard-working skill by:

1.
2.
3.
4.
5.

DAILY SCRIPTURES ON: THE BENEFITS OF HARD-WORKING

(*To guide you and inspire you as you go about your daily business*)

DAY I: "*Whatever your hand finds to do, do it with all your might, for in the grave where you are going, there is neither working or planning nor knowledge nor wisdom*"(Ecclesiastes 9:10)

DAY 2: "*Diligent hands will rule, but laziness ends in a slave labour*" (Proverbs 12:24).

DAY 3: "*All hard work brings a profit, but mere talk leads only to poverty*" (Proverbs 14:23).

DAY 4: "*Go to the ants you sluggard; consider its ways and be wise! It has no commander, no overseer or ruler, yet it stores its provisions in summer and gathers its food at harvest*". (Proverbs 6:6-8)

DAY 5: "*We hear that some among you are idle. They are not busy; they are busybodies. Such people we command and urge in the Lord Jesus Christ to settle down and earn the bread they eat. As for you brothers, never tire of doing what is right*". (2 Thessalonians 3:11-13)

DAY 6: "*Do not love sleep or you will grow poor, stay awake and you will have food to spare* (Prov. 20:13)

DAY 7: "*One who is slack in his work is a brother to one who destroys*" (Proverbs 18:9).

INTEGRITY

GENERAL FEATURES

Incorruptibility

Soundness

Trustworthiness

Decency

Honesty

THE VIRTUE OF INTEGRITY BLOSSOM LIKE A FLOWER WHEN NURTURED PROPERLY

SO! MAKE A DECISION TODAY TO TAKE GOOD CARE OF IT.

VIRTUE NUMBER EIGHT: INTERGRITY

READ ON!

My office telephone rang one Monday morning. I picked it up and said:

"Coign Books, Makhukhu speaking. May I help you"?

"My name is Solomon Mothwa (not his real name) and I am a Procurement Officer for Sehlabeng municipality. We would like to place an order with your company".

"What kind of order is it?" I asked.

"Library books!'. He answered

"What is the value of your order"? I asked.

"R800 000-00 He answered.

"Send me your requirements then and I will gladly prepare a quotation and sent it back to you for consideration". I answered

Solomon Mothwa paused for a minute and then said.

"The total cost of your quotation should be R800 000-00.But my office will pay you R800 000-00 and then you pay R100 000-00 in cash back to me".

I paused for a second and then said:

"How do I balance my books at the end of the financial year then?"

"That will be your own baby". He answered

"I am a man of integrity and I run my business above board and I will never accept any business under the carpet. As much as I need money desperately, there is no way I can stoop so low to accept kickbacks business"? I answered.

He became very agitated and began to use some unpalatable words against me. But I stood my ground because I knew that the Good Lord I serve is a God of justice and fairness. I painfully lost that deal. My small company needed financial injection desperately at that time but there was no way we could sell our souls for anything. Five months after this mishap we were forced to close down our office and started operating from our home to cut down the costs. Integrity is not something you could purchase from the supermarket. You earn it through sweat and blood and there is no way you may exchange it for anything under the sun. The author of the Book of (1 Kings 9:4) emphasises the importance of walking in integrity when he said, "*If you walk before me in integrity of heart and uprightness, as David your father did, and do all*

I command and observe my decrees and laws. I will establish your royal throne over Israel forever, as I promised David your father and said 'You shall never fail to have a man on the throne of Israel'".

WHAT IS INTEGRITY

Integrity is the eighth essential virtue humans should strive to possess. Integrity means moral uprightness. Other words describing integrity are: Purity, goodness, honesty, soundness and completeness. A person of integrity is always faithful to his moral consciousness. He always keeps his word and stand up for what is believes is right. To have integrity is to become a whole person so that what you say and do in different situations is always consistent rather than contradictory. You become consistent and dependable in all you do and say. James highlighted the importance of integrity when he wrote to the early diaspora church and said, *"Let your 'yes' be 'yes' and your 'no' be no, or you will be condemned"*. A person with a reputation for exaggeration or lying often cannot get anyone to believe his word alone. Human beings should never become like that. We should always be honest so that others may believe our simple yes or no. By avoiding lies, half-truths and omissions of the truth, we will become known as trustworthy persons-people of integrity.

Blessings accompanying living in integrity and honesty are:

- You please God. When you apply integrity in your life, you please God. King David highlighted this fact in his famous prayer when he said, *"I know my God that you test the heart and are pleased with integrity. All these things have I given willingly and with honest intent. And now I have seen with joy how willingly your people who are here have given to you"* (I Chronicles. 29:17).So! Live in integrity and honesty in all you do.

- You gain a good reputation. When you live in integrity and honesty, you gain a lot of reputation among your peers, neighbours and colleagues. Kings take pleasure in honest lips, they value a man who speaks the truth.(Proverbs 16:13)

- You receive God's protection. "He holds victory in store for the upright; he is a shield to those whose walk is blameless". (Proverbs 2:7).Pride and greed have destroyed May innocent life. They are still continuing to sow seed of hatred and mistrust all over the world. But if we are faithful and keep our purpose in life clearly in mind, he will keep us from pride and greed.

- You gain security for yourself. If ever we needed two powerful forces to preserve us along life's way, they are integrity and uprightness. Uprightness says, *"This is the shepherd's way"* and integrity says, *"Will walk consistently in it"*. King David emphasised this fact very strongly when he said, *"May integrity and uprightness protect me, because of my hope in you"* (Psalm 25:21).

- You gain security for future generation. When you live in integrity and honestly, you are actually planting a seed of success and prosperity for your children and you children's children. God promised king David and said, *"I will establish your royal throne over Israel forever, as I promised David your father when I said, You shall never fail to have a man on the throne of Israel"*(1 Kings 9:5). God kept his promise and kept the kingdom of Israel safe and strong for many years. The author of the Book of Exodus (20:6) sums it up as follows; *"But I show love to a thousand generations of those who love me and keep my commandments"*.

JOSEPH: MAN OF INTEGRITY

Joseph was a man of integrity with very strong beliefs. He did not allow the circumstances of his time to shake his faith and made him to lose focus about the real issues. The strength of what we believe is usually measured by how much we are willing to suffer for those beliefs. And Joseph was a perfect example in this regard. He was a man of integrity with strong unshakable beliefs. He was prepared to do what was right, despite the pain he knew would cause. When Mary told him about her pregnancy, Joseph knew that the child was not his. His respect for Mary's character and the explanation she gave him, as well as her attitude towards the expected child, have made it hard to think his bride had done something wrong. Still, someone else was the child's father-and it was mind-boggling to accept that the "someone else "was God. He decided he had to break the engagement. But he was determined to do it in a way that would not cause public shame to May. He intended to act with justice and love.

Perhaps Joseph thought he had only two options; divorce Mary quietly, or have her stoned. None of these two reasons was a perfect solution to the problem at hand. But God had the third option-marry her. God sent a message to Joseph to confirm Mary's story and open another way of obedience for Joseph-to take Mary as his wife. Joseph obeyed God; married Mary and honoured her virginity until the baby was borne. We do not know how long Joseph lived his role as Jesus' earthly father. But from the look of things, he did very well as a father and leader. He trained his son in the trade of carpentry; made sure he had good spiritual training in Nazareth and took the whole family to Jerusalem for the Passover which Jesus continued to observe during his adult years.

Joseph was a man of integrity. His actions revealed four admirable qualities:

(1) Righteousness (Matt.1:19).

(11) Discretion and sensitivity (Matt 1:19)

(111) Responsiveness to God (1:24)

(1V) Self-discipline (1:25)

Although Joseph seemed to be doing the right thing by breaking the engagement, only God's guidance helped him make the best decision. God sent a messenger for Joseph-to take Mary as his wife. Joseph obeyed God; married Mary and honoured her virginity until the baby was born. This is something that is impossible to do from human perspective. But from God's perspective this is possible. We do not know how long Joseph lived his role as Jesus earthly father. He is last mentioned when Jesus Christ was 12 years old. But Joseph trained his son in the trade of carpentry, made sure that he had good spiritual training in Nazareth and took the whole family on the yearly trip to Jerusalem for the Passover. This was a great responsibility to organise such a trip, but Joseph organised it annually without fail. When our decisions affect the lives of others, we must always seek God's wisdom. We should place God first in our decision-making process and he will surely lead us all the way. Joseph's story is told in (Matthew 1, 16-22:23, Luke 1:26-2:52)

LIFE-SKILLS LESSONS FROM INTEGRITY

We may draw the following lessons from this most important eighth virtue. These are:

- INTEGRITY IS REQUIRED IN BUSINESS DEALINGS: *"Honest scales and balance are from the Lord; all the weights in the bag are of his making"* (Prov.16:1).Whether you buy or sell, make a product of offer a service you know what is honest and what is dishonest. Sometimes you feel pressure to be dishonest in order advance yourself or gain more profit. But if you want to obey God. There is no middle ground because God demands integrity through and through.

- INTEGRITY IS EXPECTED FROM CHRISTIAN LEADER: *"Similarly, encourage the young men to be self-controlled. In everything set them an example by doing what is good. In your teaching show integrity, seriousness and soundness of speech that cannot be condemned, so that those who oppose you may be ashamed because have nothing bad to say about us"* Titus 2:6-7). When Paul encouraged Titus and through Titus other young men, to be serious, he wanted them to be reverent and purposeful. They should young men whose characters and behaviours are always underpinned by integrity. However they should not let the seriousness of the Gospel cause them to repel others by their disposition.

- INTEGRITY IS EXPECTED OF THE UPRIGHT: *"The integrity of the upright guides them, but the unfaithful are destroyed by their duplicity"* (Proverbs 11:3).God encourages all Christians not to be deceitful or be involved id double-dealings. Being a person of integrity will definitely help you to be above reproach in all the departments.

- INTEGRITY IS PREFERRED ABOVE WEALTH: *"Better a poor man whose walk is blameless than a rich man whose ways are perverse"* (Proverbs 28:6).Living a life of integrity is better than all the riches the world may offer to you. Remember! All the riches and wealth is going to disappear when you ultimately return back to your Maker and what you will remain with will be your integrity. So! Live a life of integrity.

- INTEGRITY IS LINKED WITH OBSERVING ALL GOD'S COMMANDS. *"As for you walk before me in integrity of heart and uprightness, as David you Father did, and do all I command and observe my decrees and laws"* (1 Kings 9:4).If you observe God's commands in all you do, you will never fail. But the same is true if you do not. Solomon did not observe God's commands and he died a shameful death and his kingdom was divided into two kingdoms.

SELF-ASSESSMENT ON INTEGRITY

GIFTING	LOW	AVERAGE	GOOD
• My Incorruptibility skill is?			
• My Trustworthiness skill is?			
• My Soundness skill is?			
• My Honesty skill is?			
• My Decency skill is?			

ACTION POINTS

I will improve and maintain my integrity by:

1.	
2.	
3.	
4.	
5.	

DAILY SCRIPTURES ON: BENEFITS OF INTEGRITY

(To guide you and inspire you as you go about your daily business)

- DAY 1:*"Have you considered my servant Job? There is no one on earth like him; he is blameless and upright, a man who fears the Lord and shuns evil. And he is still maintaining his integrity. Though you incited me against him to ruin him without any reason"* (Job 2:3).

- DAY 2: *"I know my God that you test the heart and are pleased with integrity. All these things have I given willingly and with honest intent. And now I have seen with joy how willingly your people who are here have to you"* (1 Corinthians 29:17).

- DAY 3: *"And David shepherded them with integrity of heart with skilful hands he let them"* (Psalm 78:72).

- DAY 4:*"They did not require an accounting from those to whom they gave the money to pay the workers, because they acted with complete honesty"* ((2 Kings 12:15).

- DAY 5: *"I put in charge of Jerusalem my brother Hanani along with Hananiah the commander of the cidetal because he is of integrity and feared God more than men do"* (Nehemiah 7:2).

- DAY 6: *"Teacher" they said. "We know you are a man of integrity and that you teach the way of God in accordance with the truth. You aren't swayed by men, because you pay no attention to who they are"* (Matthew 22:16).

- DAY 7: *"The man of integrity* walks *securely, but he who takes crooked paths will be found* out" (Proverbs 10:9)

GRATITUDE

GENERAL FEATURES

Thankfulness

Gratefulness

Appreciation

Recognition

Acknowledgement

THE VIRTUE OF GRATITUDE BLOSSOM LIKE A FLOWER WHEN NURTURED PROPERLY

SO! MAKE A DECISION TODAY TO TAKE GOOD CARE OF IT.

VIRTUE NUMBER NINE: GRATITUDE

READ ON!

September 1972 will always remain a milestone in my life. I was baptised into the African Methodist Episcopal church and the South African Council of Churches offered me a bursary to go and register for my Senior Certificate at Setotolwane high school. This was a real life saver for me because I could not further my studies due to my disadvantaged background. John Rees allocated me Student Number (C19) which allowed me an opportunity to further my studies. Stringent conditions were attached to the bursary though. I did not disappoint. I used this bursary for the next five years until I completed my university degree at the end of 1977.I then received a one year government bursary to complete my University Education Diploma. All in all I received six years quality education without my parents paying anything. I am very grateful. This will remain a real miracle.

I wrote a letter to the South African Council of Churches in January 1979, firstly thanking them and then asked them how I should pay them back. They informed me that their financial assistance was a free bursary and I was very thankful. I was over the moon. The first thought that came to my mind was to offer the same opportunity to a needy person or persons. After much thought and prayer, I approached World Vision and asked them if I could adopt a needy family through their sponsorship programme. Rev. Sebe- the local World Vision Administrator in Polokwane facilitated my request. We were given one teenager-Amos Matsimela from Winterveld in Pretoria. Our family sponsored him until he completed his senior certificate examination. That was a kind of gesture I always dreamed about. The second labour of love our family did for World Vision was a big gas stove donation at their Sekororo facilities in Tzaneen. It came in at the right time and was very handy.

The gratitude spirit has always been part and parcel of my adult life since then. I inherited this kind of spirit from my mother. She was always ready to help because she came from a very poor background .Many people took care of her and she became the kind of person who always took keen interest in other people's affairs. I am always looking for an opportunity where I could help someone. In all my 18 years teaching experience I always made sure that I organised a "Guidance and Counselling Bureaux" for the professional staff and students. I achieved positive results. I finally enrolled for a Certificate in Business Mentorship and I am now practising as a professional Business Coach and I am assisting many people and businesses. A labour of love indeed! King Solomon put this important fact very clear when he said, *"He who is kind to the poor lends to the Lord, and he will reward him for what he has done"* (Proverbs 19:17).

WHAT IS GRATITUDE

Gratitude is the ninth essential virtue humans should strive to possess. Gratitude is defined as a "state of being thankful or readiness for and the ability to return kindness". It comes from the Latin word *gratus* meaning pleasing or thankfulness. It is described as a secret for a happy life. Other words describing gratitude are: Appreciation, gratefulness, acknowledgement, recognition and thanksgiving. Gratitude is a choice we make. You may choose to be thankful just as you choose to love. But you may also choose to hate just as you choose to kill and destroy. Gratitude takes away all our entitlement attitudes and tendencies and helps us to develop a godly thankful spirit.

MARY MAGDELINE: WOMAN OF GRATITUDE

Mary Magdalene was a woman of great gratitude. She was an early follower of Jesus Christ who certainly deserves to be called a disciple. She was an energetic, impulsive and caring woman. She did not only travel with Jesus Christ, but also contributed to the needs of the group. She was present at the crucifixion and was on her way to anoint Jesus 'body on Sunday morning when she discovered the empty tomb. She was the first to see Jesus after his resurrection. She went to the tomb early in the morning and saw that the stone had been removed from the entrance. So she came running to Simon Peter and other disciple, the one Jesus loved and said, "*They have taken the Lord out of the tomb, and I do not know where they put him*"!

We are not told about her background but she seems to have been very wealthy. She is a heart-warming example of thankful living. Her life was miraculously freed by Jesus Christ when he drove seven demons out of her (Mark 16:9).In every glimpse we have of her, she was acting out of her appreciation for the freedom Jesus Christ has given her. That freedom allowed her to stand to stand under Jesus Christ's cross when all the disciples except John were hiding in fear. After Jesus Christ's death she intended to give his body every respect. Like the rest of Jesus' followers, she never expected his bodily resurrection-but she was overjoyed to discover it.

Mary Magdalene's faith was not complicated, but was direct and genuine. She was more eager to believe and obey than to understand everything. Jesus Christ honoured her childlike faith by appearing to her first and by entrusting her with the first message of his resurrection. Mary Magdalene's story is told in (Matthew 27, 28, Mark 15, 16, Luke 23, 24) and John 19, 20.She is also mentioned in (Luke 8:2)

LIFE-SKILLS LESSONS FROM GRATITUDE

We may draw the following life-skills lessons from this very important ninth virtue. These are:

- DO NOT BE PICKY: Appreciate everything. Gratitude starts with appreciating every good thing in life and recognising that there is nothing too small for you to be thankful for. Even if it is as simple as appreciating the clear weather. Do not leave anything out of your sphere.

- FIND GRATITUDE IN YOUR CHALLENGES. Gratitude is not only about being thankful for positive experiences. In fact, sometimes thinking about negative or difficult situations can help to really nail down what you have to be thankful for. Dig a little deeper into some of your own past experiences and try to figure out how they have helped shaped you into the person you are today.

- PRACTICE MINDFULNESS: Sit down daily and think through five to ten things you are grateful for. The challenge that you need to picture it in your mind and sit with that feeling of gratitude in your body. Doing this every day will rewire your brain to be naturally more grateful and you will start feeling happier after every session. Start today.

- VOLUNTEER: For many people, the key to having more gratitude is to give back others in their local community. Not only will it make you more grateful for the things that you take for granted, but studies have shown that volunteering for purpose of helping others increases our own well-being, and thus our ability to have more gratitude.

- SPENT TIME WITH LOVED ONES: If you are struggling with feeling gratitude in the moment, go spend time with your friends and family. It will help you to grow closer to them and strengthen your relationship, but it will also give you a chance to act your acts of gratitude on people that you care about.

- IMPROVE YOUR HAPPENINGS IN OTHER AREAS OF YOUR LIFE: Being grateful can make you happy, but being happy can also make you grateful. There are other ways to get your mood up, including exercising or participating in a hobby you enjoy. Once you are feeling the endorphins flow, showing gratitude will become easier and you will start to be able to make list after list of all the things in your life you are thankful for.

SELF-ASSESSMENT ON GRATITUDE

GIFTING	LOW	AVERAGE	GOOD
• My thankfulness skill is?			
• My gratefulness skill is?			
• My appreciation skill is?			
• My recognition skill is?			
• My acknowledgement skill is?			

ACTIONS POINTS

I will improve and maintain my gift of gratitude by:

1.	
2.	
3.	
4.	
5.	

DAILY SCRIPTURES ON GRATITUDE

(To guide you and inspire you as you go about your daily business)

- DAY 1: *"I will give thanks to the Lord because of his righteousness and will sing praise to the name of the Lord Most High"* (Psalm 7:17).

- DAY 2: *"I will praise you Lord, with all my heart; I will tell of all your wonders. I will be glad and rejoice in you; I will sing praise to your name Most High"* (Psalm 9:1-2).

- DAY 3: *"Speak to one another with psalms, hymns and spiritual songs. Sing and make music in your heart to the Lord. Always giving thanks to God the Father for everything, in the name of our Lord Jesus Christ"* (Ephesians 5:19-20)

- DAY 4: *"Do not be anxious about anything, but in everything, by prayer and petition, with thanksgiving, present your requests to God. And the peace of God which transcends all understanding will guard your hearts and minds in Christ Jesus"* (Philippians 4:6-7).

- DAY 5: *"Therefore, since we are receiving a kingdom that cannot be shaken, let us be thankful, and so worship God acceptably with reverence and awe… (Heb.12:28-29).*

- DAY 6: *"We rejoice in our suffering, because we know that suffering produces perseverance. Perseverance, character, and character, hope. And hope does not disappoint us, because God has poured out his love into our hearts by the Holy Spirit, whom he has given us"*(Romans 5:3-5).

- DAY 7: *"Therefore we do not lose heart. Though outwardly we are wasting away, yet inwardly we are being renewed day by day. For our light and momentary troubles are achieving for us an eternal glory that far outweighs them all".* (2 Corinthians 4:16-17)

HUMILITY

GENERAL FEATURES

Humbleness

Modesties

Meekness

Diffidence

Mildness

THE VIRTUE OF HUMILITY BLOSSOM LIKE A FLOWER WHEN NURTURED PROPERLY

SO! MAKE A DECISION TODAY TO TAKE GOOD CARE OF IT

VIRTUE NUMBER TEN: HUMILITY

READ ON!

Queen Esther was a humble woman and her humility and beauty were her strongest weapons. Her name means "Myrtle". She was a beautiful and humble young Jews who grew up in Susa, the capital of Persia. She was an orphan, cared for by her cousin Mordecai. Esther" beauty, humility and character won king Xerxes' heart and he made his queen. Even in her favoured position, however she would risk her life by attempting to see the king when he had not requested her presence. There was no guarantee that the king would even see her. Although she was queen, she was still not secure. But humbly, cautiously and courageously, Esther decided to risk her life by approaching the king on behalf of her people

She made her plans carefully and played her cards very close to her chest. She asked the Jews to fast and pray with her before she went to the king. Then on a chosen day she went before him, and the king did ask her to come forward and speak. This was unusual occurrence indeed. Call it a miracle or an unusual incident because it never happened in the kingdom of Persia before. But instead of issuing her request directly, she invited the king and his trusted commander, Haman to a banquet. King Xerxes was astute enough to realise that Queen Esther had something on her mind, yet she humbly and cautiously conveyed the importance of her matter by insisting on a second banquet.

In the meantime, God was working behind the scenes. He caused king Xerxes to read the historical records of the kingdom late one night and the king discovered that Mordecai (Queen Esther's cousin) had once saved his life. King Xerxes lost no time in honouring Mordecai for that act. During the second banquet, Esther told the king of Haman's plot against the Jews and Haman was doomed There is grim justice in Haman's death on the gallows he had built for Mordecai, and it seems fitting that the day on which the Jews were to be slaughtered became the day their enemies died. The Bible says, *"It is not good to punish an innocent man, or to flock officials for their integrity"*. (Proverbs 17:26).Queen Esther's character and humility won the day. Esther story is told in the book of Esther.

WHAT IS HUMILITY

Humility is the tenth essential virtue humans should strive to possess. Humility means having or showing a low esteem of one's own importance. Other words describing humility are: Humbleness, modesty, meekness, submissiveness and simplicity. A humble person is able to recognise both his inadequacies and abilities but then choose to press his abilities and potentialities into useful services without intending to attract attention or expecting a reward. Humility involves

- A CHILDLIKE ATTITUDE. God want us to develop a *childlike* faith. *Childlike* attitude is good but *childish* attitude is not good for our spiritual growth. That is why Jesus rebuked his disciples and said, *"I tell you the truth, unless you change and become like little children, you will never enter the kingdom of heaven. Therefore whoever humbles himself like this child is the greatest in the kingdom of heaven"*. (Matthew 18:1-4).We are not to be *childish* (like the disciples arguing over petty issues), but rather *childlike*, with humble and sincere hearts.

- SUBMISSION BEFORE GOD. Humility allows us the opportunity to humble ourselves before God. King Hilkiah submitted himself before the Lord when the Book of the Law was read to him and the Lord said to him, *"Because your heart was responsive and you humbled yourself before God when you heard what he spoke against this place, and because you have humbled yourself before me and tore your robes and wept in my presence, I have heard you, declares the Lord".* *(2 Chronicles 34:27)*

- SUBMISSION INVOLVES FOLLOWING GOD'S LAWS: Humility involves following God's laws and decrees without fail. God spoke to Israel through prophet Jeremiah and said, *"To this day they have not humbled themselves or shown reverence, nor have they followed my law and the decrees I set before you and your fathers"*(Jeremiah 44:10).To fail to learn from failure is to assure future failures. Our past is our school of experience and we should hold on dearly what we have learnt so that we could not repeat the same mistakes again.

- WORKING FOR JUSTICE AND MERCY: Humility involves working for justice and mercy. In his case against Israel, the Lord made his wishes very clear. He wanted his people to be just, merciful and to walk humbly with him. He spoke through prophet Micah and said, *"God has shown you man, what is good. To act justly and to love mercy and to walk humbly with your God".* ((Micah 6:8)

- HUMILITY IS THE OPPOSITE OF PRIDE: *"Young men, in the same way be submissive to those who are older. All of you cloth yourselves with humility toward one another"* (1 Peter 5:5) Peter told both young and old to be humble and to serve each other. Young men should follow the leadership of the older men and should lead by an example. Respect the elderly.

CORNELIUS: THE HUMBLE CENTURION

Cornelius means a "horn". He was a godly humble and a generous Roman centurion. A Centurion was a commander of 100 soldiers. He was a Gentile and a Roman citizen. His humility stemmed from the fact that he responded to the Good News about Jesus Christ while stationed in Judea. Because of the frequent outbreaks of violence in Israel, Roman soldiers had to be stationed at every corner to keep peace throughout Israel. Cornelius was deployed to Israel together with other soldiers. He was occupying a very senior position in the military. But most of the Roman soldiers did not get along well with the Israelites. As an officer, Cornelius was in a difficult position. He represented the Roman government and his home was in Caesarea. During his years in Israel, he had himself been conquered by the God of Israel. He became a very prayerful man. He had a reputation of a godly humble man who put his faith into action. And he was respected by the Jews.

Four significant aspects of Cornelius' humble character are noted in the book of Acts. He actively sought God and he revered God (Acts 10:30-33).He was always generous in meeting other people's needs and he prayed God. In one of his prayers God told him to send for Peter, because Peter would give him more knowledge about the God he was seeking to please. He welcomed Peter at his house with open hands. Peter had not sooner started sharing the gospel when God gave overwhelming approval by filling that Roman family with the Holy Spirit. Cornelius and all his family were devout and God-fearing. He gave generously to those in need and prayed to God regularly.

Cornelius and Peter were very different people. Cornelius was a wealthy, a Gentile, and a military man. Peter was a Jewish fisherman turned preacher. But God's plan included both of them. In Cornelius' house that day, a new chapter in Christian history was written as Jewish Christian leader and Gentile Christian convert each discovered something significant about God at work in the other person. Cornelius needed Peter and his Gospel to discover the way to salvation. Peter needed Cornelius and his salvation experience to know that Gentiles were included in God's plan too. Today the door of salvation is open to all the people across the world without and limitation or restriction. Cornelius' story is told in (Acts 10:1-11:18).

LIFE-SKILLS LESSONS

We may draw the following lessons from this very important tenth virtue. These are:

- GOD GUIDES AND TEACHES THE HUMBLE. The Bible says *"He guides the humble in what is right and teaches them his way"* (Psalm 25:9).We are bombarded today with relentless appeals to go in various directions. Television advertising alone places hundreds of options before us. In addition to appeals made by political parties, cults, false religions and dozens of other groups etc., we find ourselves continuously pulled in different directions. But humility keep us stable and focused all the way.

- GOD HOLDS THE HUMBLE IN ESTEEM: The Bible says, *"Has not my hand made all these things, and so they came into being"* (Isaiah 66:2).God shows mercy to the humble, but he curses the proud and self-sufficient (see Luke 1:51-53).Our society urges us to be assertive and to affirm ourselves. We should not let our freedom and right to choose lead us away from God's pathway to eternal life.

- GOD BLESS THE HUMBLE: *"If my people, who are called by my name, will humble themselves and pray, and seek my face and turn from their wicked ways, then I will hear from heaven and will forgive their sins and will heal their land."*(2 Chronicles 7:14).In order to satisfy this basic requirements, God set out four basic conditions for all of us to meet: (1).We must humble ourselves by admitting our sins. (11).We must pray to God asking for forgiveness. (111).We must seek God continually (1v).We must turn from sinful behaviour.

- GOD REWARDS THE HUMBLE: *"Humility and fear of the Lord bring wealth and honour and life"* (Proverbs 22:4).The Book of Proverbs contains many strong statements about the benefits of wisdom, including long life, wealth, honour and peace. It describes life the way it should be and does not dwell on the exceptions.

- GOD SAVES THE HUMBLE: *"You save the humble but bring low those whose eyes are haughty"* (Psalm 18:27).God is indeed a shield to protect and save us when we are too weak to face certain trials by ourselves, but he does not want us to remain weak. He saves, strengthens, protects and guides us in order to send us back into an evil world to fight for him. And then he continues to work with us because the strongest person on earth is infinitely weaker than God and needs his help.

- GOD RECEIVES THE LOWLY: God spoke through Isaiah and said, *"I will not accuse forever, nor will I always be angry, for then the spirit would grow faint before me and the breath of man that l have created. I was enraged by his sinful greed. I punished him and hid my face in anger"* (Isaiah 57:16-17).

SELF-ASSESSMENT ON HUMILITY

GIFTING	LOW	AVERAGE	GOOD
• My thankfulness skill is?			
• My gratefulness skill is?			
• My appreciation skill is?			
• My recognition skill is?			
• My acknowledgement skill is?			

ACTION POINTS

I will improve and maintain humility by:

1.	
2.	
3.	
4.	
5.	

DAILY LESSONS ON HUMILITY

(To guide you and inspire you as you go about your daily business)

- DAY 1:*"Do nothing out of selfish ambition or vain conceit, but in humility consider others better than yourself Each of you should not should look not only to your own interest, but also to the interests of others"* (Philippians 2:3-4).

- DAY 2:*"When pride comes, then comes disgrace, but with humility comes wisdom"* (Pro. 11:2).

- DAY 3:*"Live in harmony with one another. Do not be proud, but be willing to associate with people of low position. Do not be conceited"* (Romans 12:16).

- DAY 4:*"Humble yourselves before the Lord, and he will lift you up"* (James 4:10).

- DAY 5:*"Your beauty should not come from outward adornment, such as braided hair and the wearing of gold jewellery and fine clothes. Instead, it should be that your inner self, the unfading beauty of a gentle and quite spirit, which is of great worth in God's sight".*(1 Peter 3-4)

- DAY 6:*"Therefore, as God's chosen people, holy and dearly loved, cloth yourselves with compassion, kindness, humility, gentleness and patience"* (Colossians 3:12).

- DAY 7:*"The fear of the Lord is the beginning of wisdom and the knowledge of the Holy One is understanding"* (Proverbs 9:10).

TERMINOLOGY

VIRTUE NUMBER ONE: WISDOM

Solomon: The son of David and Bathsheba and the third king of Israel

Rehoboam: The son of and Naamah the Ammonitess and the first king of the Southern kingdom

Moses: The leader of the Israelites in the Exodus from Egypt and their wondering to the Promised Land

VIRTUE NUMBER TWO: JUSTICE

Penge Mine: Former Asbestos mine in Sekhukhune land area

Seshego: Black township situated west of Polokwane City

Polokwane: Capital of the Limpopo Province

Nathan: The prophet and a contemporary of David.

David: Israel's second and greatest king

Bathsheba: King David's favourite wife and the mother of King Solomon

Zechariah: One of the twelve Israel's Minor Prophets

VURTUE NUMBER THREE: INTERGITY

Robben Island: Former South African political prisoners' jail

Mveso village: Nelson Mandela's birth place

abaThembu: Eastern Cape Xhosa ethnic group

Paul Kruger: Former president of the Republic of South Africa

Paul: The Apostle and founder of numerous churches, author of the 13 books of the New Testament

Stephen: A Christian Jew from Diaspora who lived in Jerusalem and was stoned to death for his faith

Gamaliel: An outstanding Pharisee, scholar and teacher. Paul was one of his pupils

Pharisees: Members of the three major parties in Judaism from the last centuries B.C. until the destruction of the Second Temple in A.D.70

Damascus: Capital of Syria in the ancient times

Tarsus: The city in Asia Minor and the birthplace of Apostle Paul

Timothy: Traveling companion and the fellow worker of Pau. The native of Lystra

VIRTUE NUMBER FOUR: SELF-CONTROL

White River: A town in Mpumalanga Province

Simon Peter: One of the twelve apostles of Jesus Christ

Joseph: Son of Jacob. The Gospels refers to him as Jesus' father

Potiphar: One of King Pharaoh's officers

Eli: High priest and judge of Israel at Shiloh for 40 years

Shiloh: A town in Mount Ephraim. Eli and his sons officiated was at Shiloh.

Philistines: One of the Sea People, who appeared at the end of the late Bronze age in the South-eastern sector of the Mediterranean

Tabernacle: The portable shrine that the Israelites took with them into the desert, made by Moses according to God's command

Dan: The fifth son of Jacob and the firstborn of Bilhah, Rachel's maid

Beersheba: A town in the Negeb, prominent in the history of the patriarchs

VIRTUE NUMBER FIVE: LOVE

Mother Teresa: Albanian-Indian Roman Catholic nun and missionary

Macedonia: The Northern part of modern day Greece, stretching from the Adriatic to the Aegean Sea

Albania: A country in Southeast Europe

Skopje: A capital and largest city in Macedonia

Dublin: A capital and largest city in Ireland

Calcutta: A large city in India

Vatican City: A city-state surrounded by Rome Italy and is the headquarters of the Roman Catholic Church

Pope Francis: The head of the Roman Catholic Church

Ruth: A Moabite woman married to one of Naomi and Elimelech's sons

Naomi: Elimelech's wife and the mother of Mahlon and Chilion

Boaz: A wealthy Bethlemite landowner and Ruth's husband

Rahab: A prostitute who played a key role in the conquest of Jericho

Moab: The land that lies to the east of the Dead Sea between Edom and Ammon

Thessalonica: She is now called Saloniki (Salonica) and is the capital of Macedonia

VIRTUE NUMBER SIX: POSITIVE ATTITUDE

Nick Vujicic: International speaker and president of the Non-profit organisation-Life Without Limps.

Melbourne: A city in Australia

Utopia: An imagined place or stage of things in which everything is perfect

Antioch: An ancient Greek city on the eastern side of the Orontes River

Barnabas: An Apostle and colleague of Paul on his first missionary journey

Jerusalem: Ancient capital of the Kingdom of Israel, located in the Judean hill range

John Mark: The writer of second of the four Gospels in the New Testament canon.

Silas: A leading member of the first Christian community in Jerusalem and a colleague of Paul

VIRTUE NUMBER SEVEN: HARD-WORKING

Priscilla: The wife of Aquila. She is also referred as Prisca (11 Timothy 4:19)

Aquila: A Jew and a native of the province of Pontus in Asia Minor. Priscilla's husband

Pontus: The coastal strip of the Northern Asia Minor bordering the Black sea and extending to the west from the Halys River to the highlands of Armenia in the east

Claudius: Roman emperor (ruled A.D. 41-54)

Corinth: The magnificent city situated on the Isthmus joining the Peloponnese to Greece commanding two seas, the Corinthian Gulf and the Saronic Gulf

Rome: The capital city of Italy

Apollos: A Jew of Alexandria, who was well versed in the scriptures and was an eloquent speaker

Luke: A doctor and traveling-companion of Apostle Paul

Amphipolis: A city of Macedonia about 3 miles (5km) from Aegean Sea and about 30 miles (48 km) southwest of Philippi

VIRTUE NUMBER EIGHT: INTEGRITY

Mary: Jesus Christ's mother

Joseph: Jesus Christ's father

Nazareth: The small town in Galilee where Jesus spent his childhood and youth

Passover: The first of the three major festivals in the Jewish liturgical calendars

Hanani : a shorter form of Hananiah

James: The author of the Epistles of James. He was Jesus Christ's brother

VIRTUE NUMBER NINE: GRATITUDE

Setotolwane. Former Institution of higher learning (30km) west of Polokwane city

Winterveld: Black settlement area Northwest of Pretoria

Pretoria: Capital city of the Republic of South Africa

World vision: International well-fare organisation

Mary Magdeline: A woman from Magdala in Galilee, who having set free from evil spirits became a faithful follower of Jesus Christ.

VIRTUE NUMBER TEN: HUMILITY

Mordecai: A Benjamite, cousin and Queen Esther's foster-father

Esther: Queen, cousin and adopted daughter of Mordecai

Xerxes: King and Esther's husband

Susa or Shushan: She (Shush today) was the capital of Elam

Haman: The main antagonist of the Jews in the Book of Esther

Cornelius: A Roman centurion stationed at Caesarea the capital of the Roman Judea Province

COIGN FOUNDATION (PTY) LTD.

Coign Foundation (Pty) Ltd. Publishing and ministry group was launched officially on 01-08-2000.Coign means "A favourable position for observation or action". This name popped out miraculously during our registration process and it was the only name we used for our company process. The DTI (Department of Trade and Industry accepted it without any question. The normal practice in business registration process is, you submit three suggested names for consideration. But in our case this one name did the trick. It is the most appropriate name for our Christian Publishing House. Our products and services include:

- Book Design and Publishing services

- Christian self-publishing services

- Christian Art and Framing services

- Marriage preparation and counselling services

OUR MISSION STAYEMENT

Our mission is to assist in the spiritual development of our people by producing and distributing consumer driven, Christ centred products and services which fosters saving faith, increasing Bible understanding and promoting the application of Christian values in everyday life.

OUR VISION

Our vision is to research and identify spiritual, educational and social needs of our people and respond with wide range of distinctive, exceptional and compelling products and services that will result in observable change in personal behaviour.

OUR PUBLISHING PHILOSOPHY STATEMENT

Our publishing philosophy is to produce Evangelical Christian Literature, Christian Art and other related materials and services which promotes, encourages, confirms, defends or establish the individual in his or her belief-all to the glory of our Lord and King, Jesus Christ

To learn more about our products and services contact

Coign Foundation (Pty) Ltd.

P.O. Box 16333

FLORAPARK 0699

POLOKWANE

RSA

CELL: 083 440 5941/083 395 5383

E-MAIL:makhukhutladi@gmail.com

OTHER BOOKS BY MAKHUKHU JOHN TLADI

COMMON DESTINY CHILDREN'S SERIES

- The Story of Creation

- Jacob's Sons: Part 1,11,111

- Clay pot: Part 1,11,111

- Kleipot:Deel 1,11,111

- Moeta: Padisho karolo ya 1

- Virtues Blossom like Flowers: Part 1

- Splendour: Birds Part 1

- Bashimane ba Mona

ARISE AND SHINE SERIES

- 12 Devious Deadly Hooks

- Tried and Tested:12 Old Testament Leaders

- Rebuilding Fallen Walls: Love, Courtship and Marriage Guide

- Right Christian Behaviour

- The Twelve Disciples

- Christian Self-publishing Made Easy

REVISITING THE PAST SERIES

- Son Not Slave: My Autobiography

- The Seed Planter: Life and Ministry of Rev. Mathole Philip Maapea:(1944-1933)

- Setlogo sa Batau

- Batau Lehono: Modern Historical Novel

- Botshela-ka-Tswati:Taodishophelo ya Rev.E.M Motubatse (1884-1986)

- Gobetse:Leshika la Magane le ShwahlaneTladi

- Creating Tomorrow's Leaders

REFERENCES

1. Sara Tulloch: The Reader's Digest Complete Word finder, Reader's Digest Association Limited, London, 1993

2. Geoffrey Wigoder et al: Illustrated Dictionary & Concordance of the Bible. The Jerusalem Publishing House Ltd.

3. The Holy Bible, New International Version, Bible Society of South Africa, Cape Town

4. Nick Vujicic: Life Without Limps,Doubleday Religion International, New York

5. Faith For Daily Living: Faith For Daily Living Foundation @2005, Durban, RSA

CPSIA information can be obtained
at www.ICGtesting.com
Printed in the USA
BVHW021145200820
586900BV00003B/55